Félix González-Torres Roni Horn

STEIDL

STEIDL

Félix González-Torres Roni Horn

with Julie Ault

for Luca

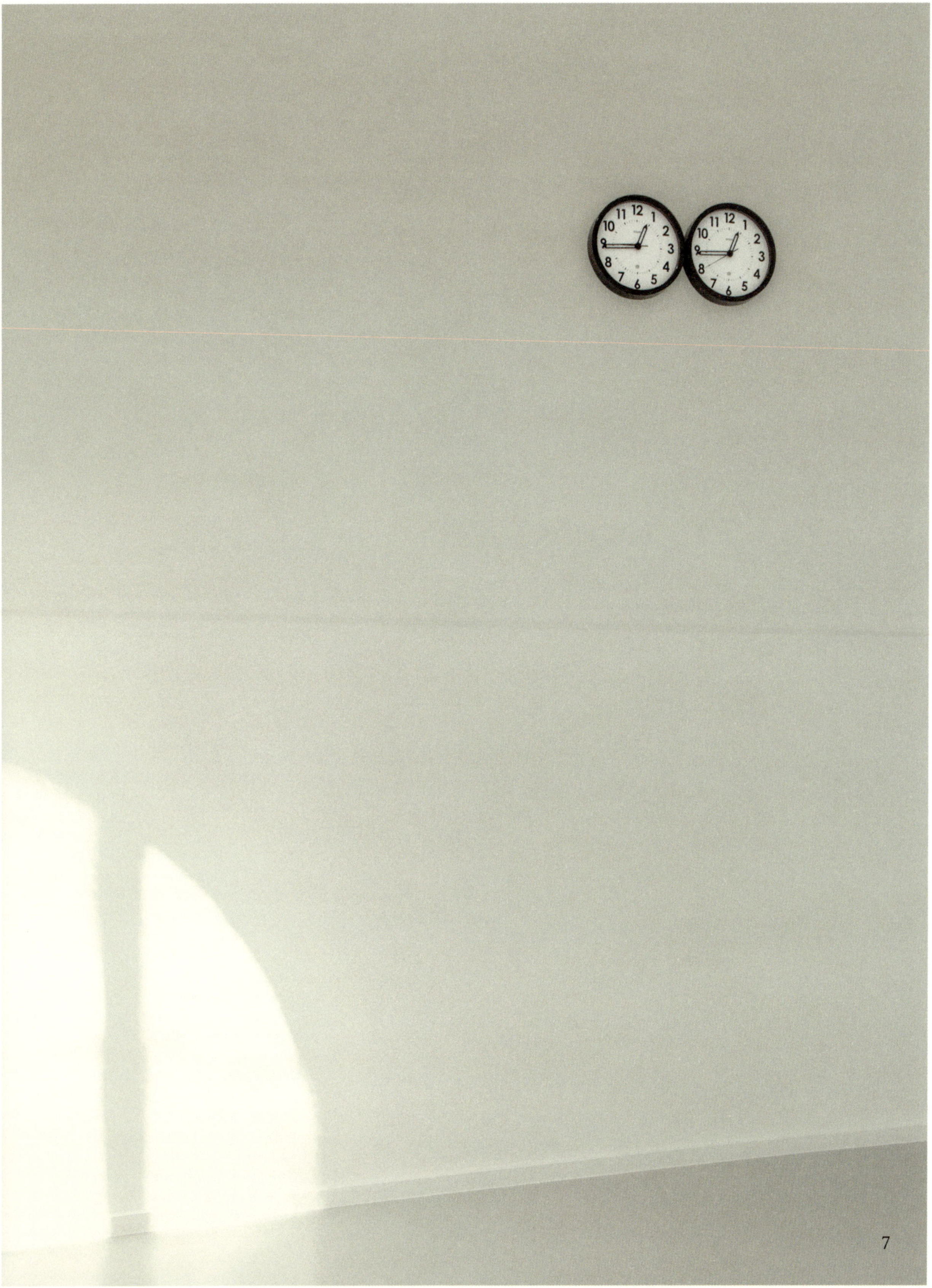

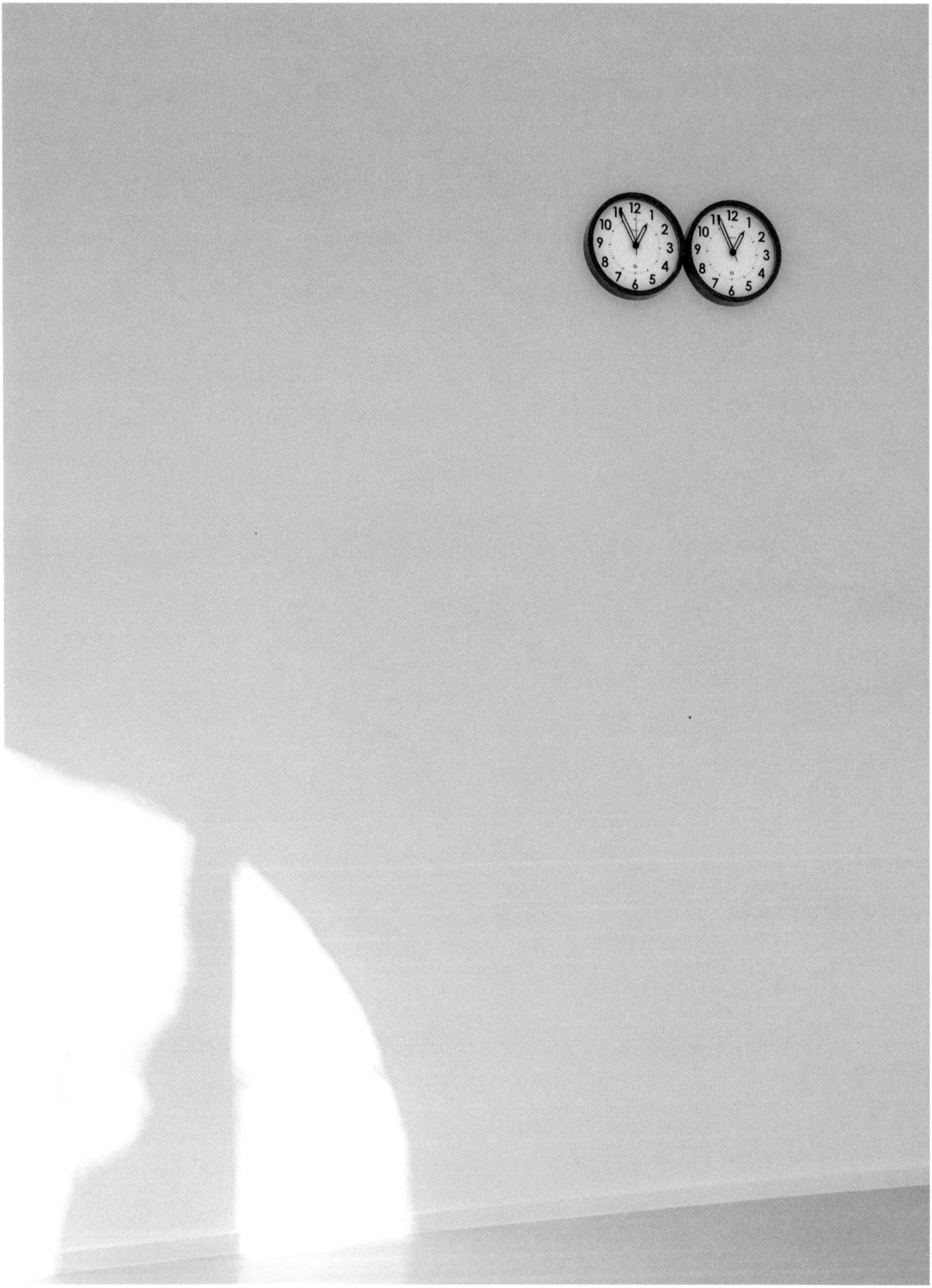

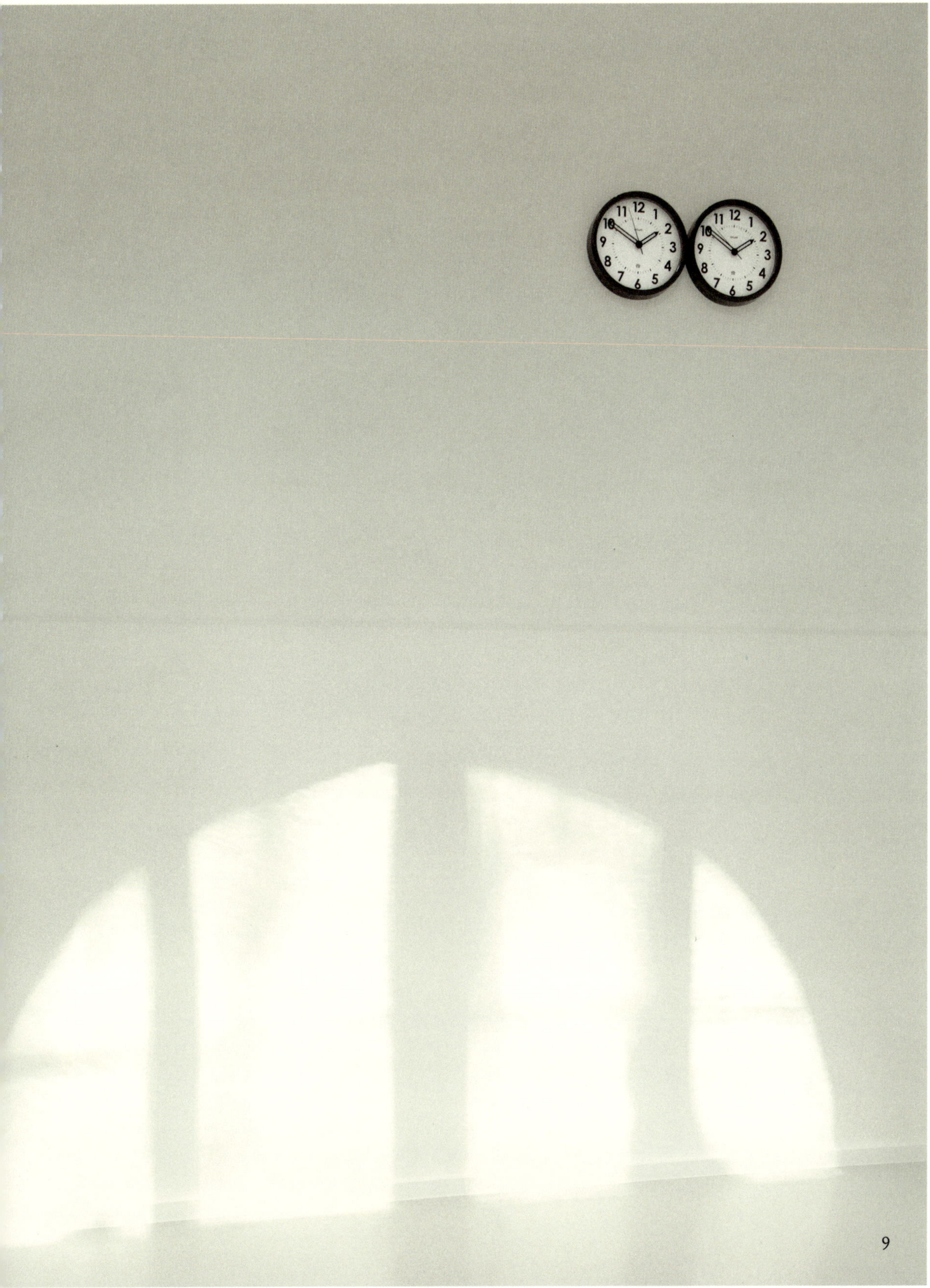

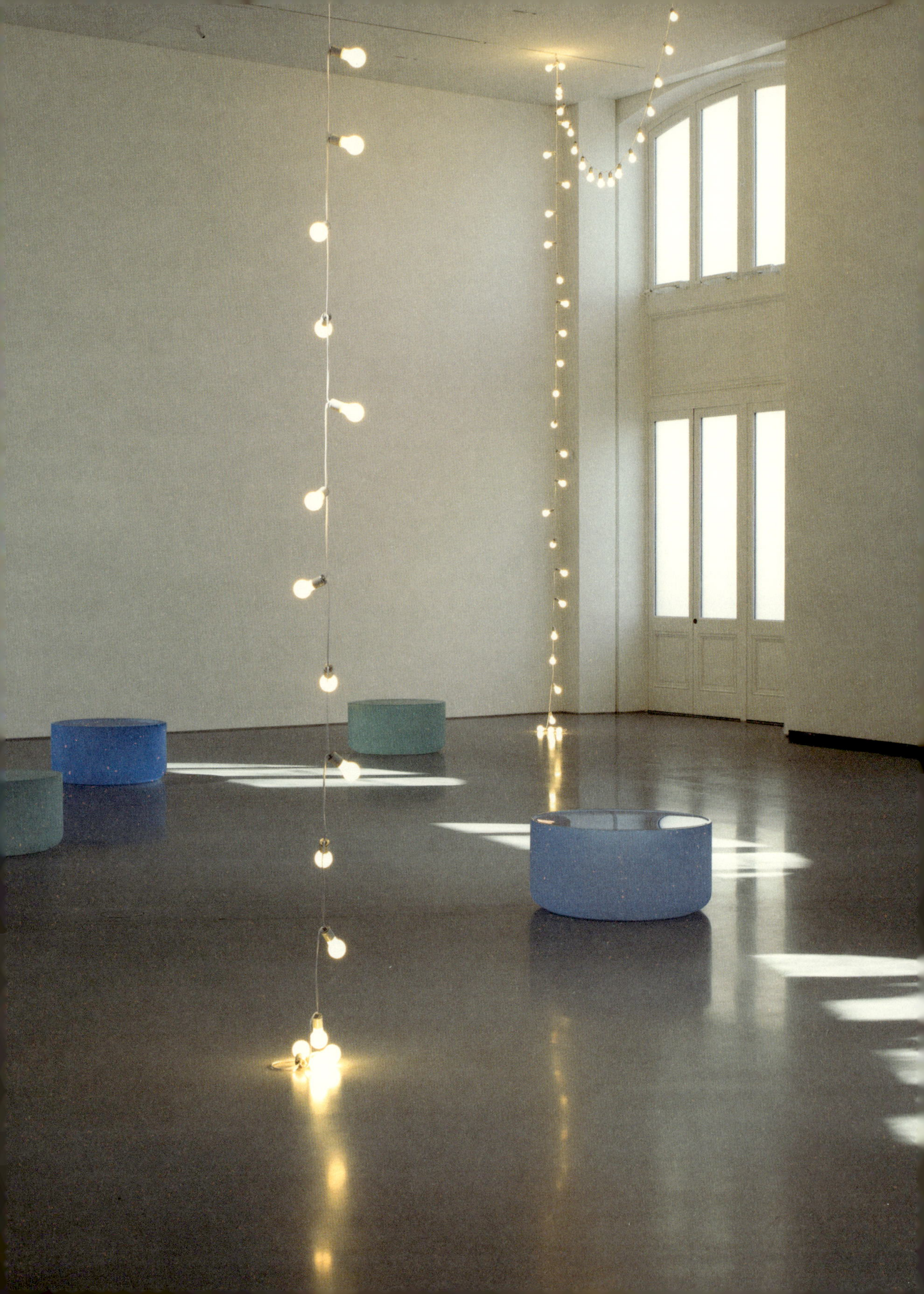

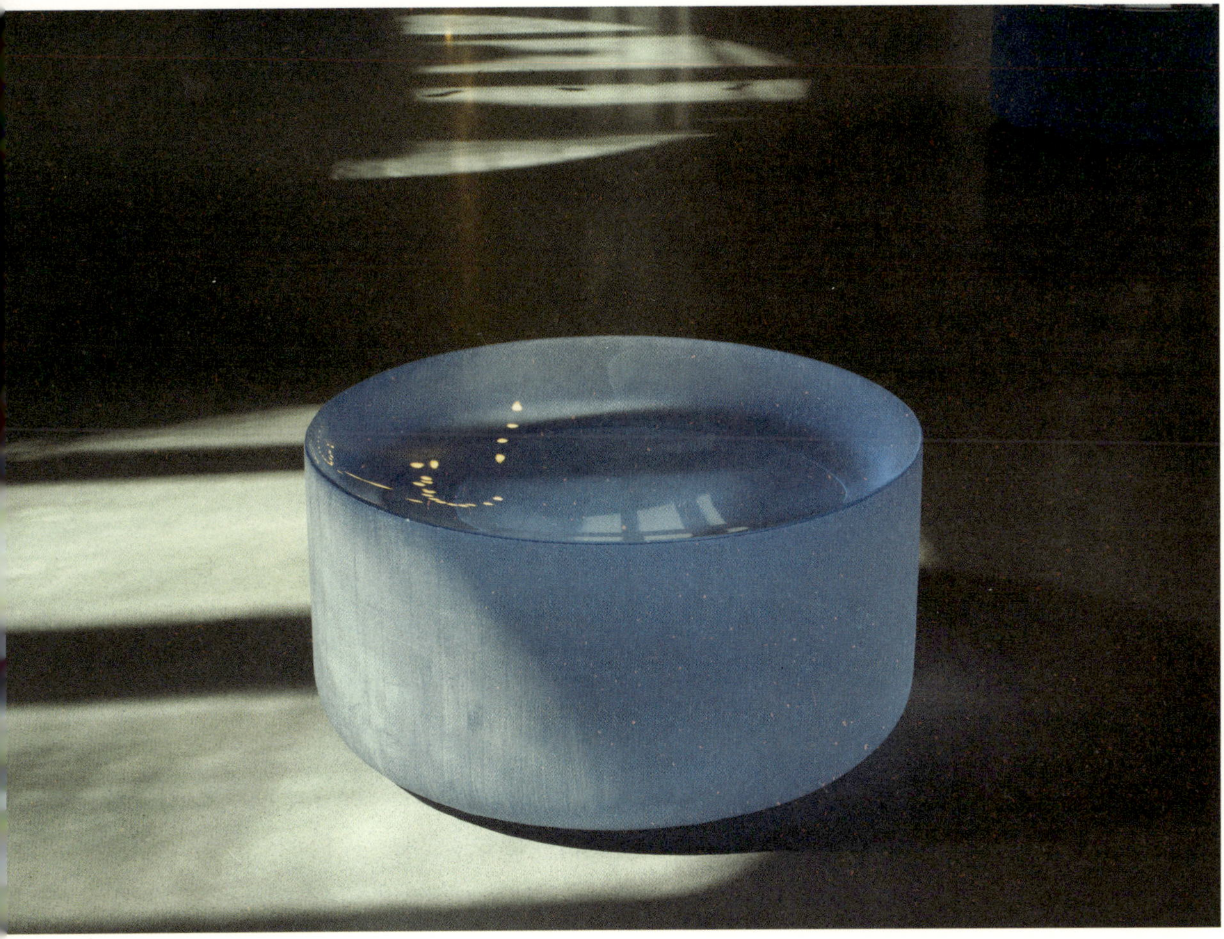

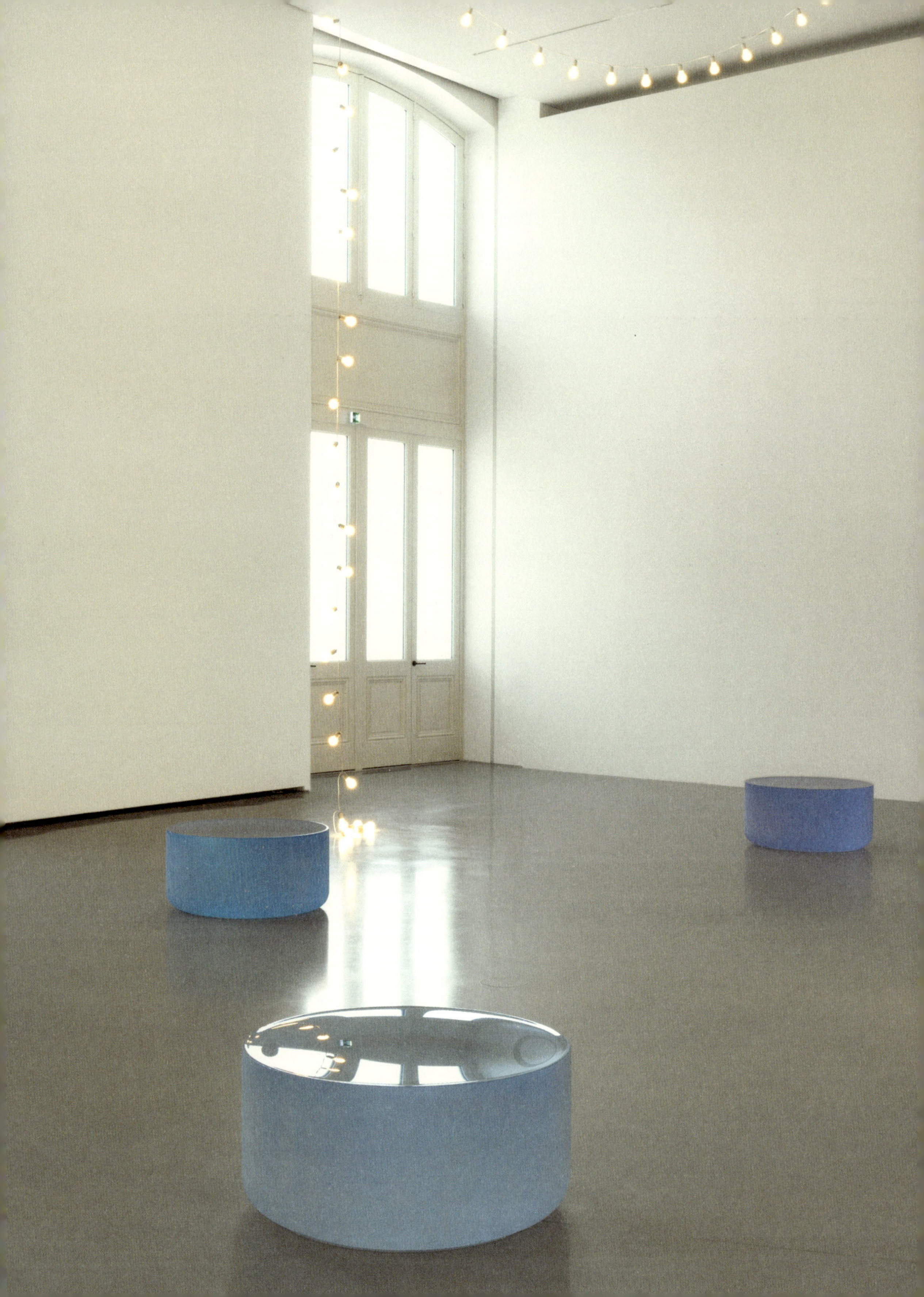

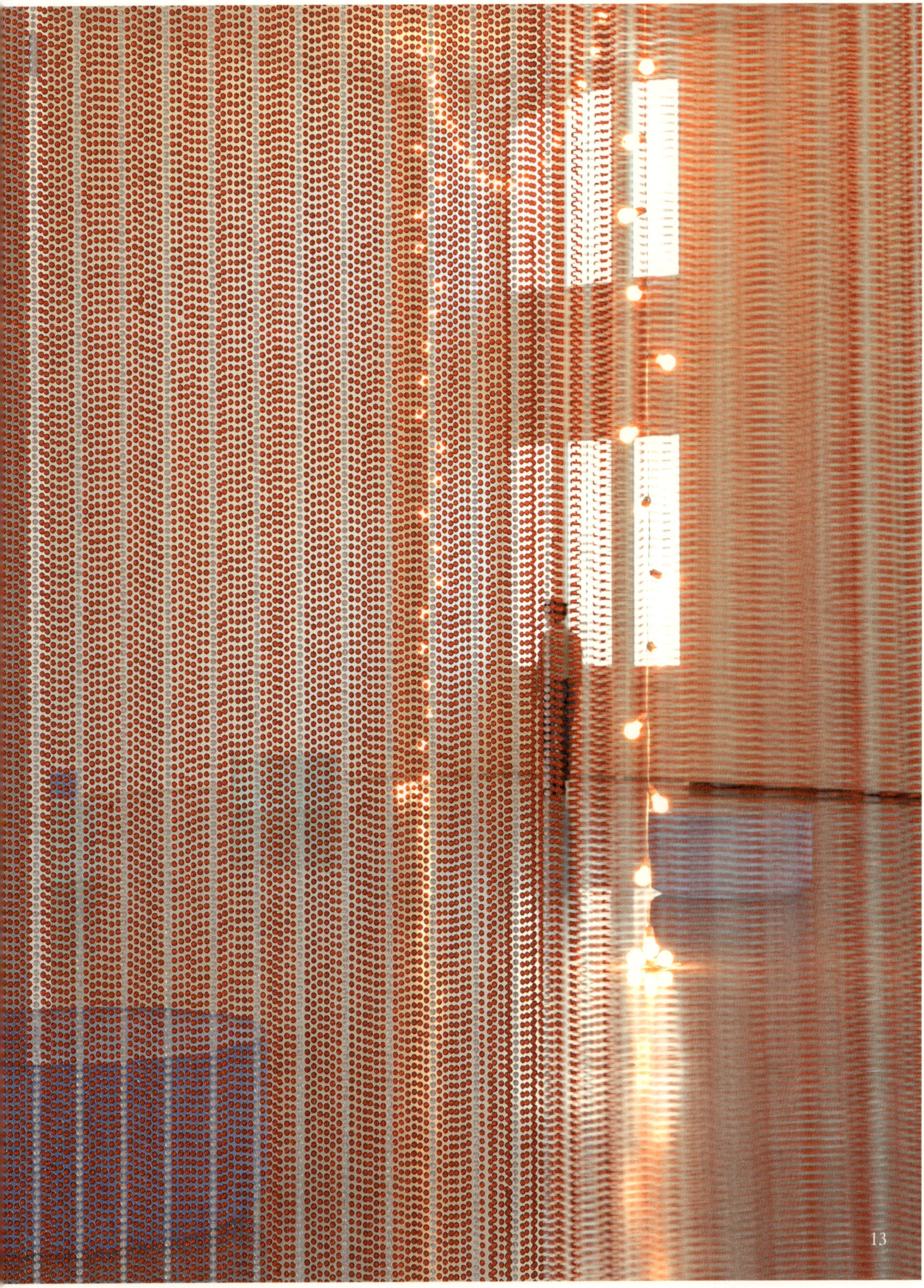

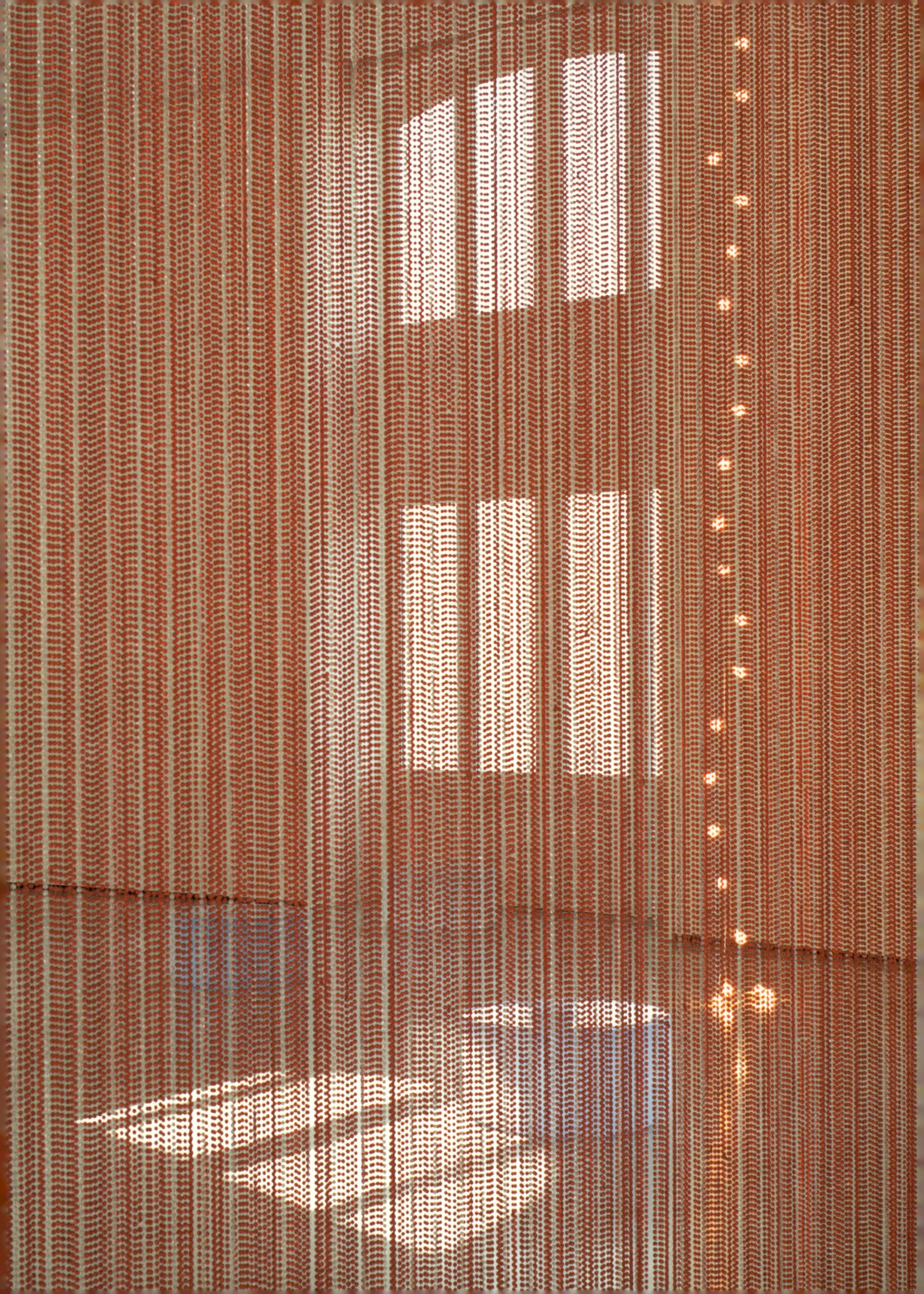

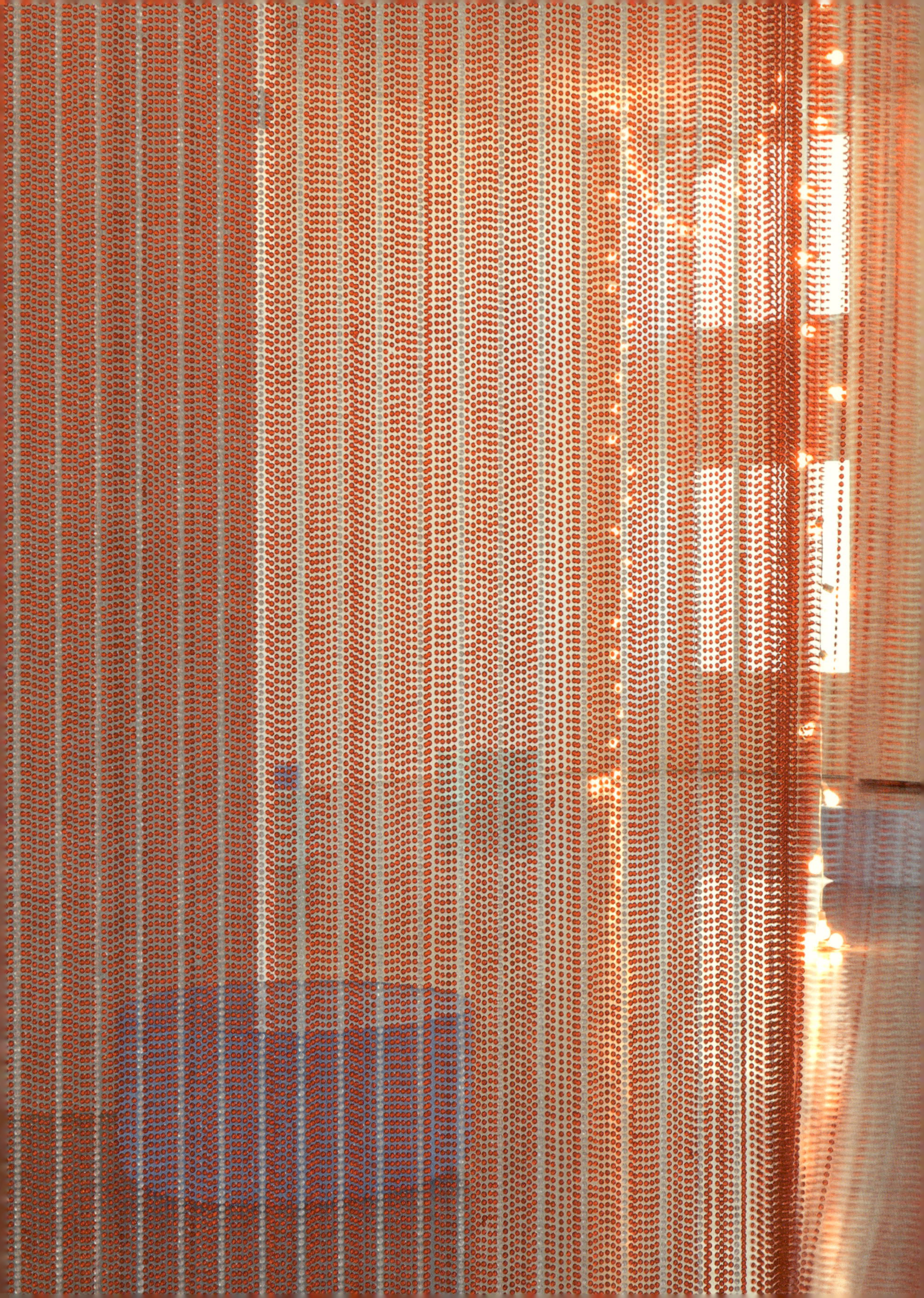

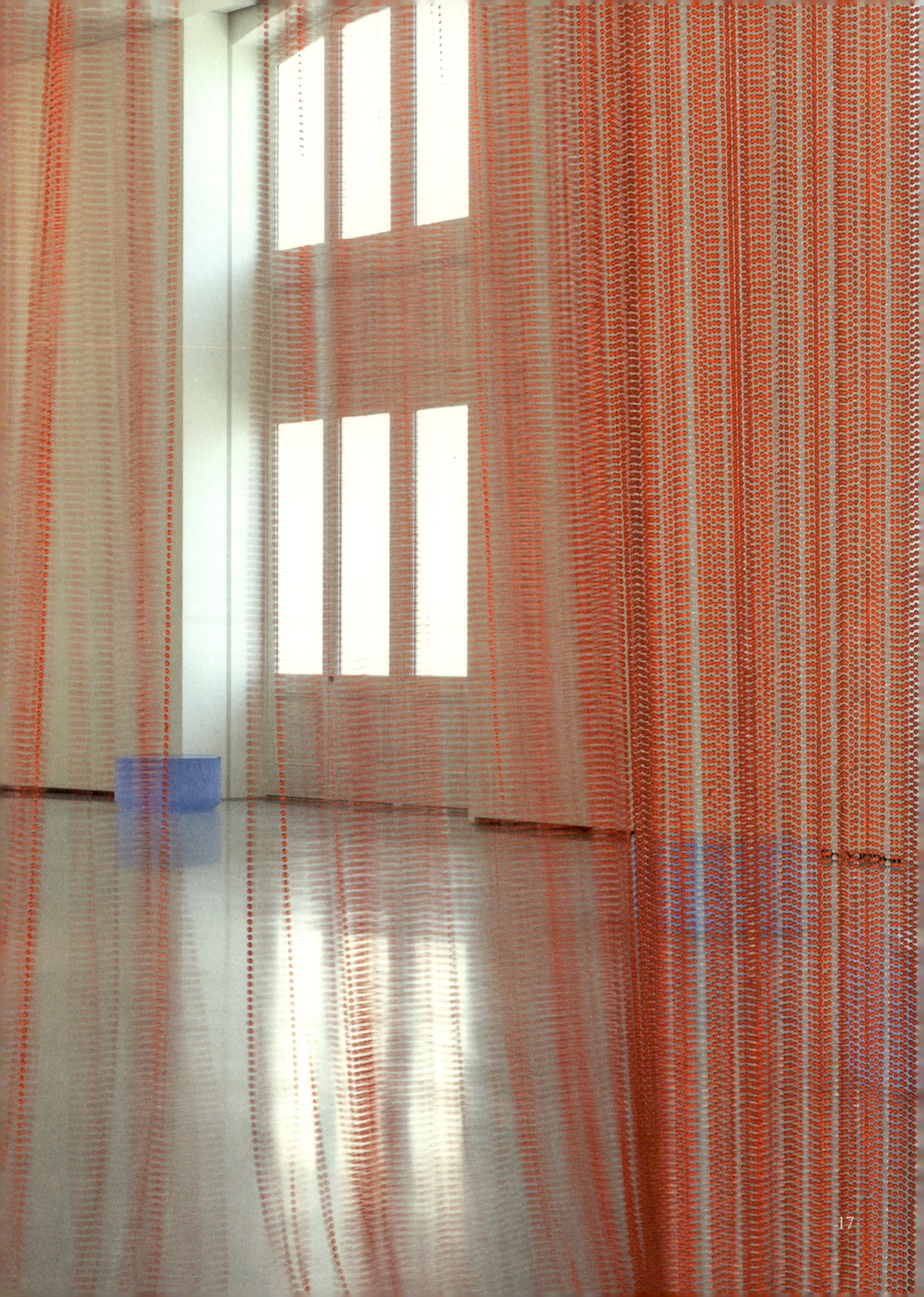

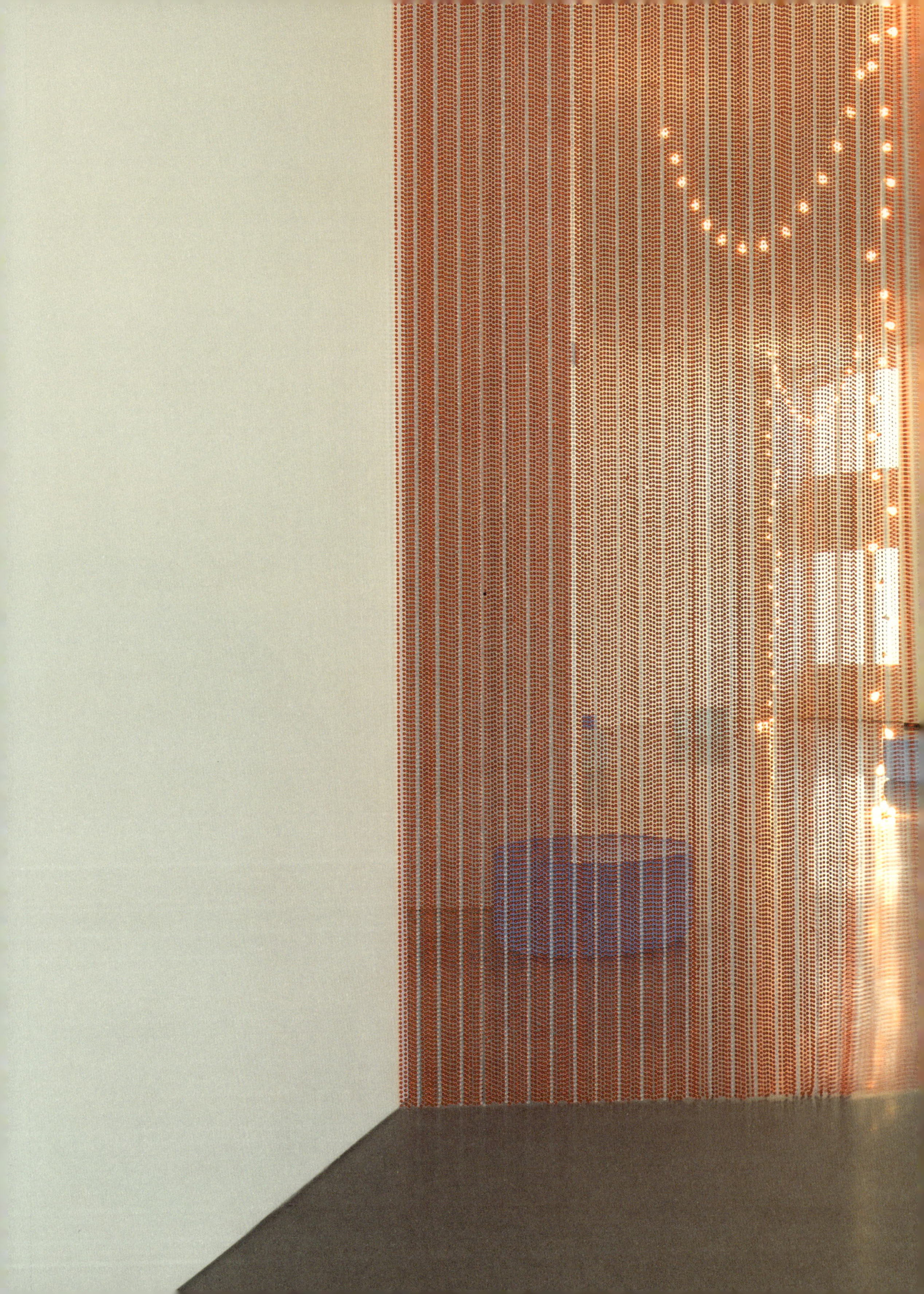

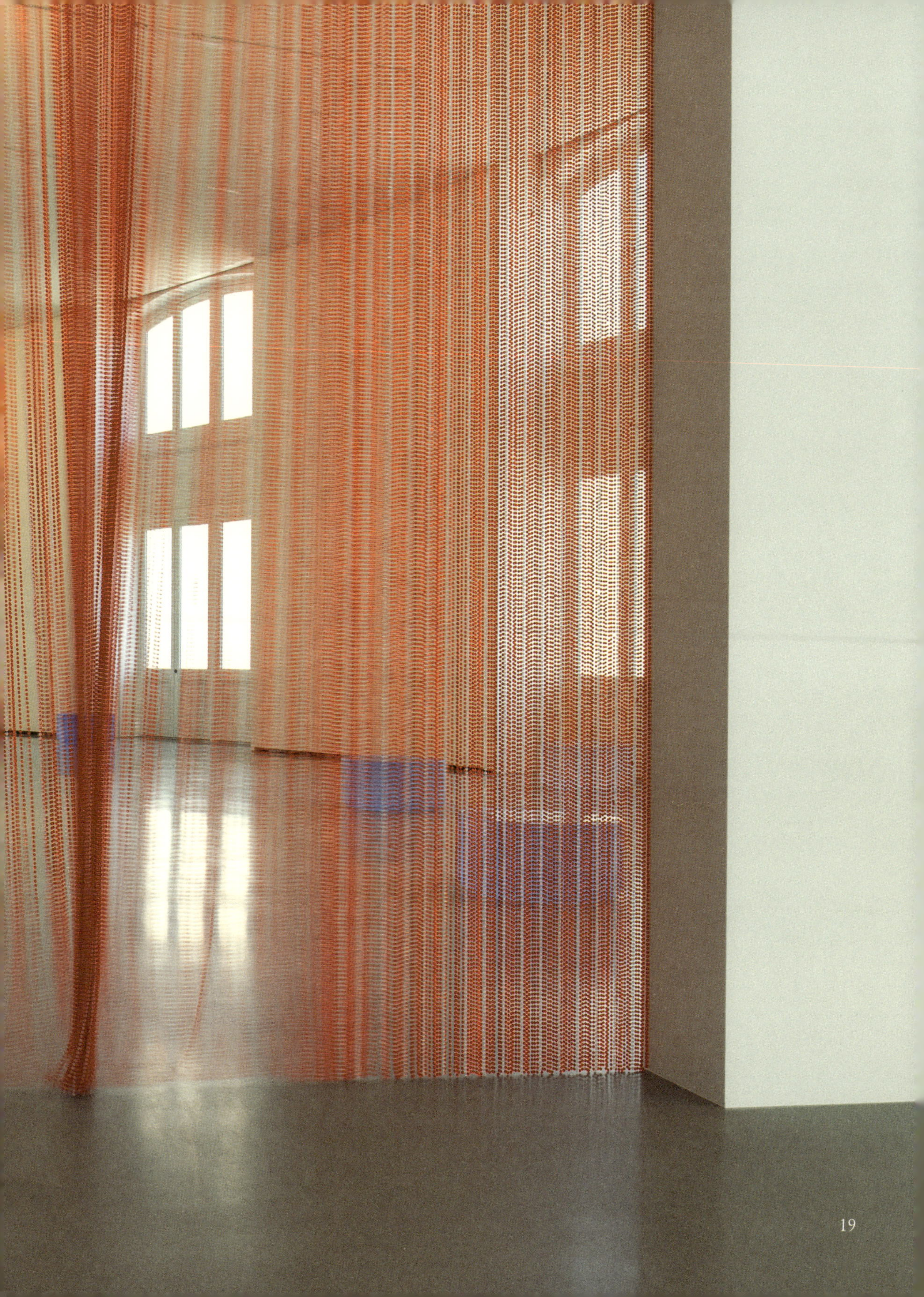

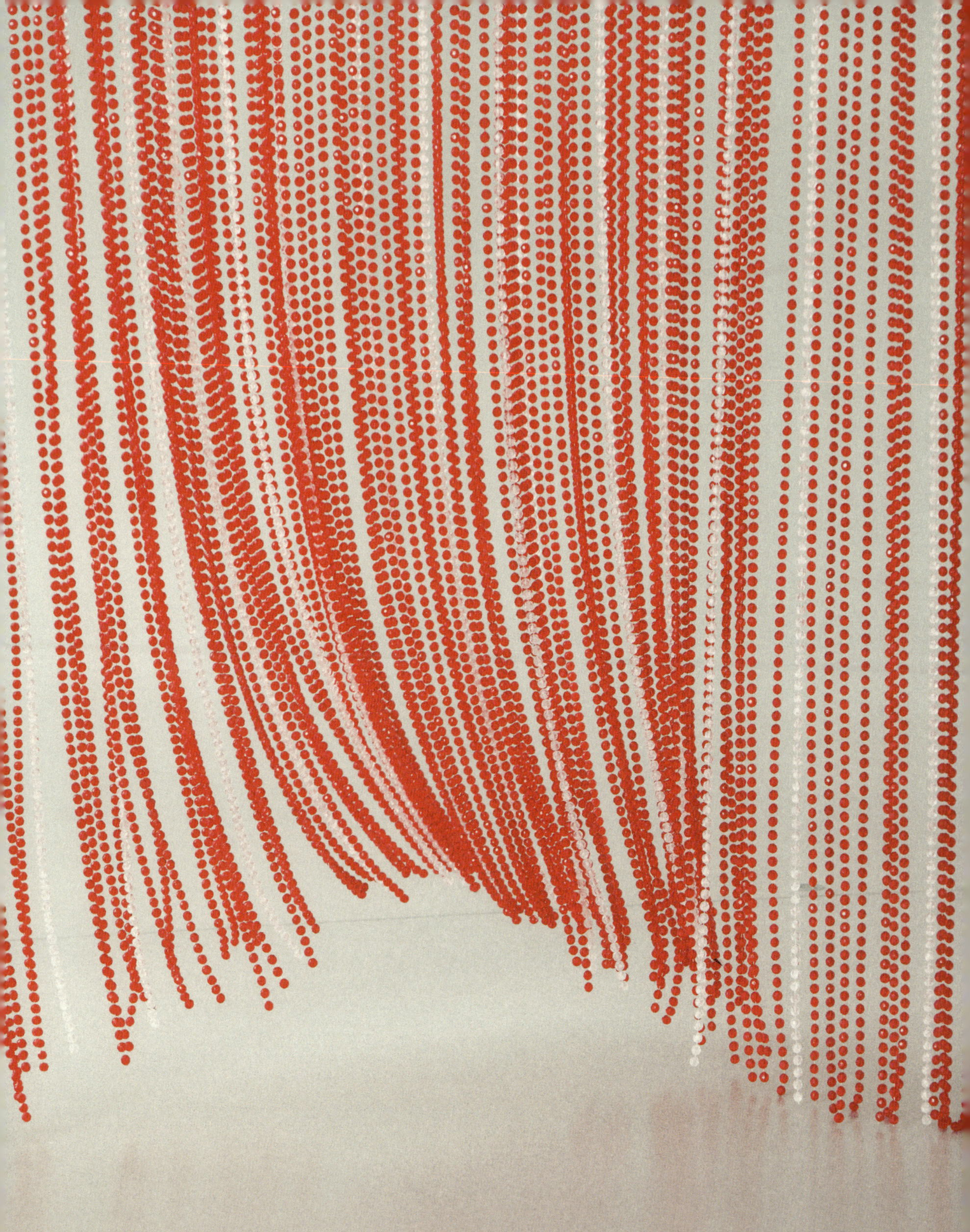

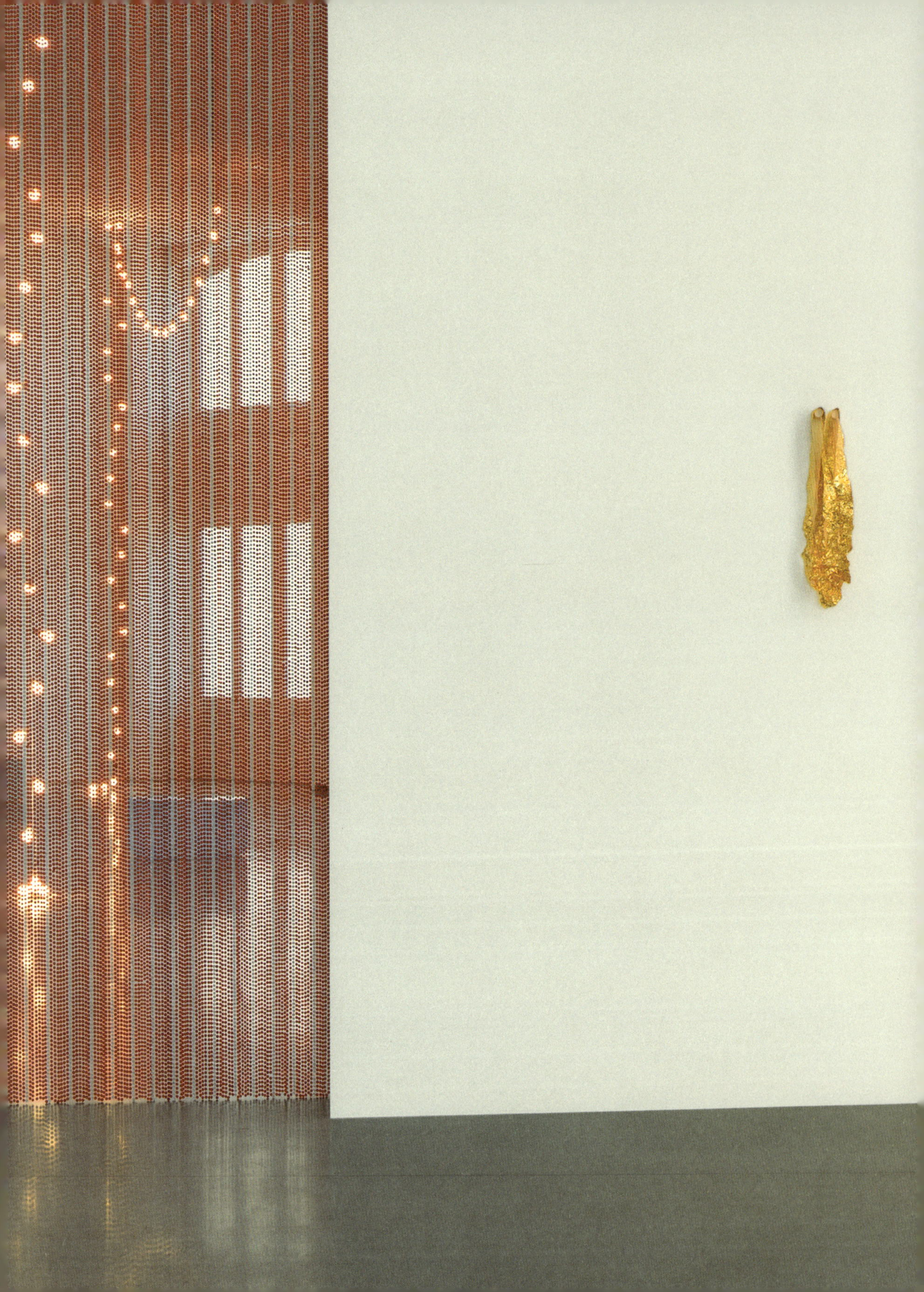

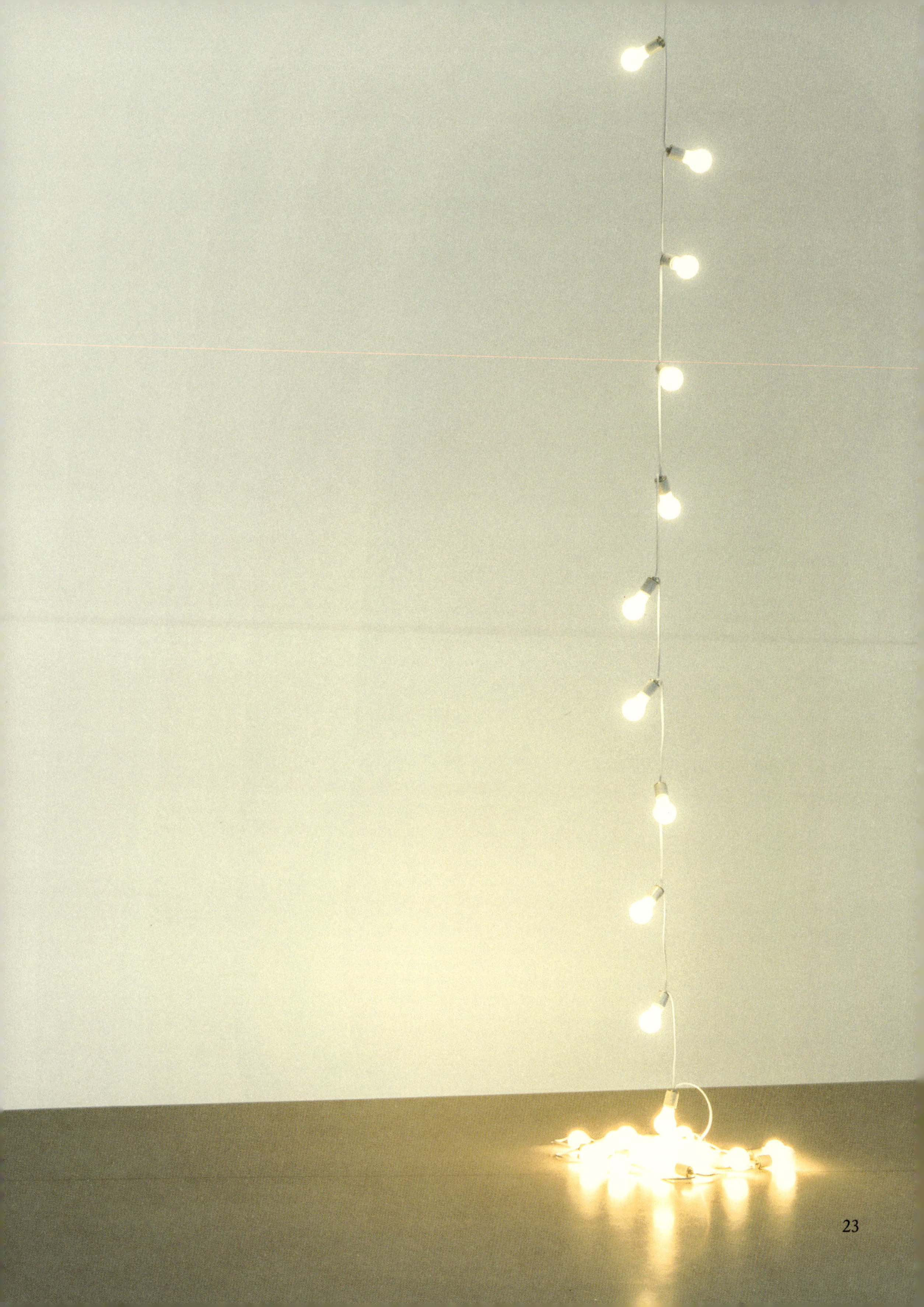

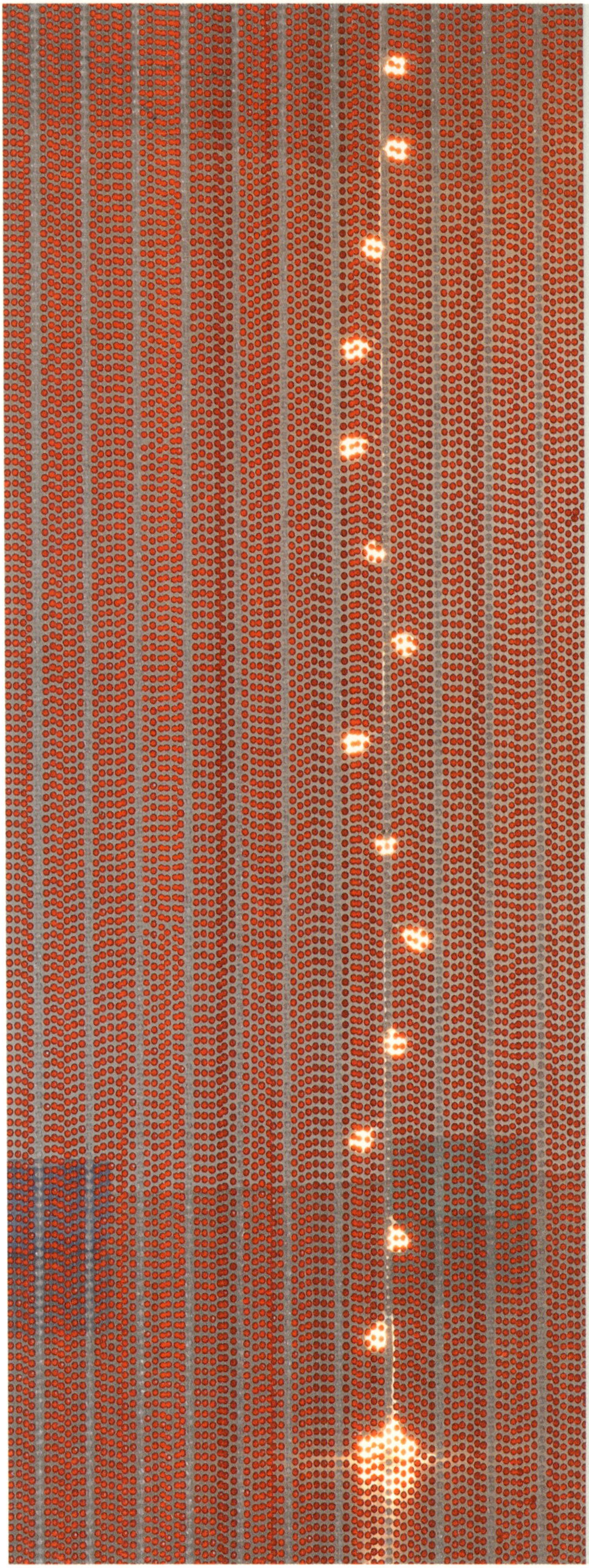

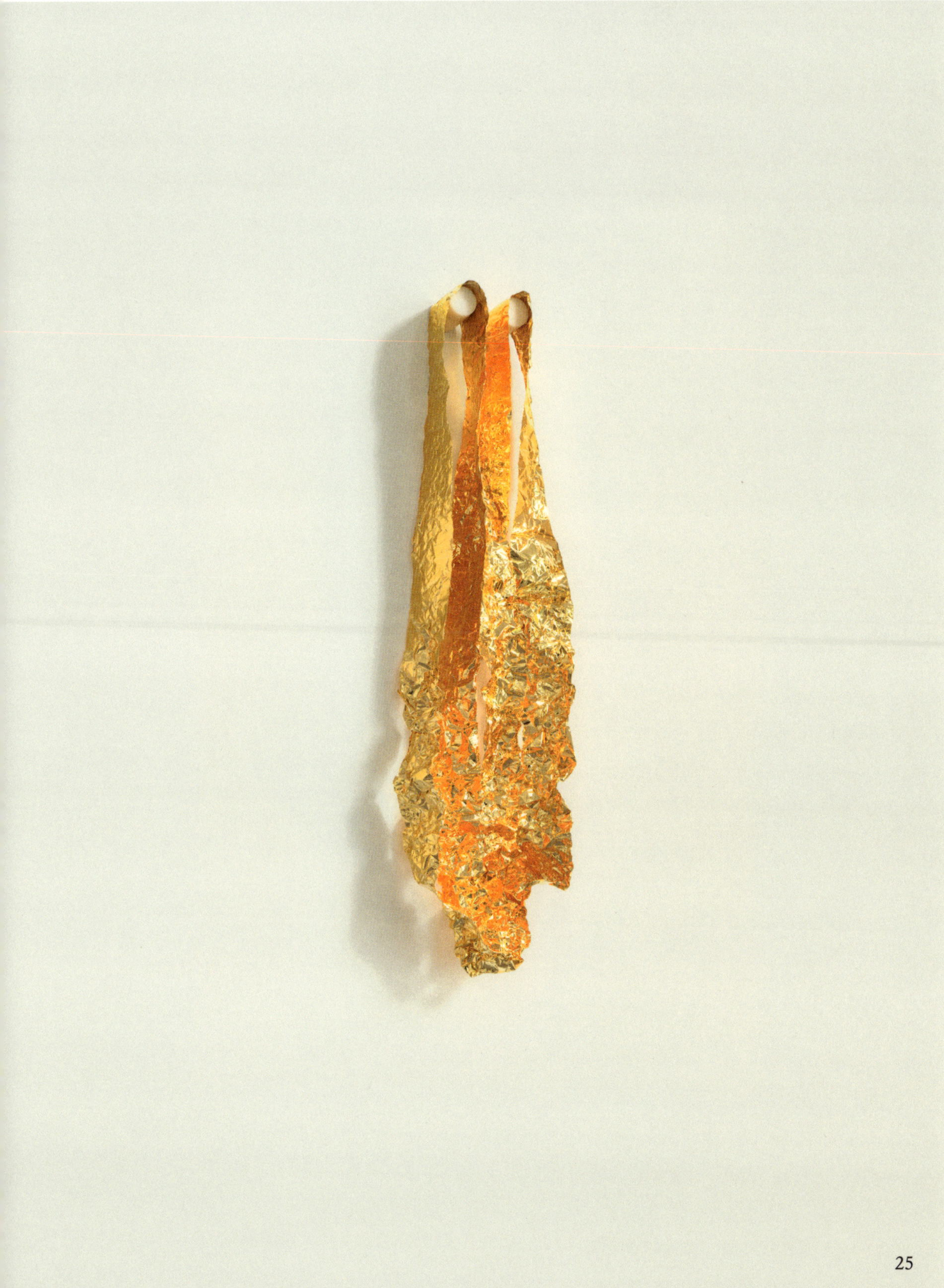

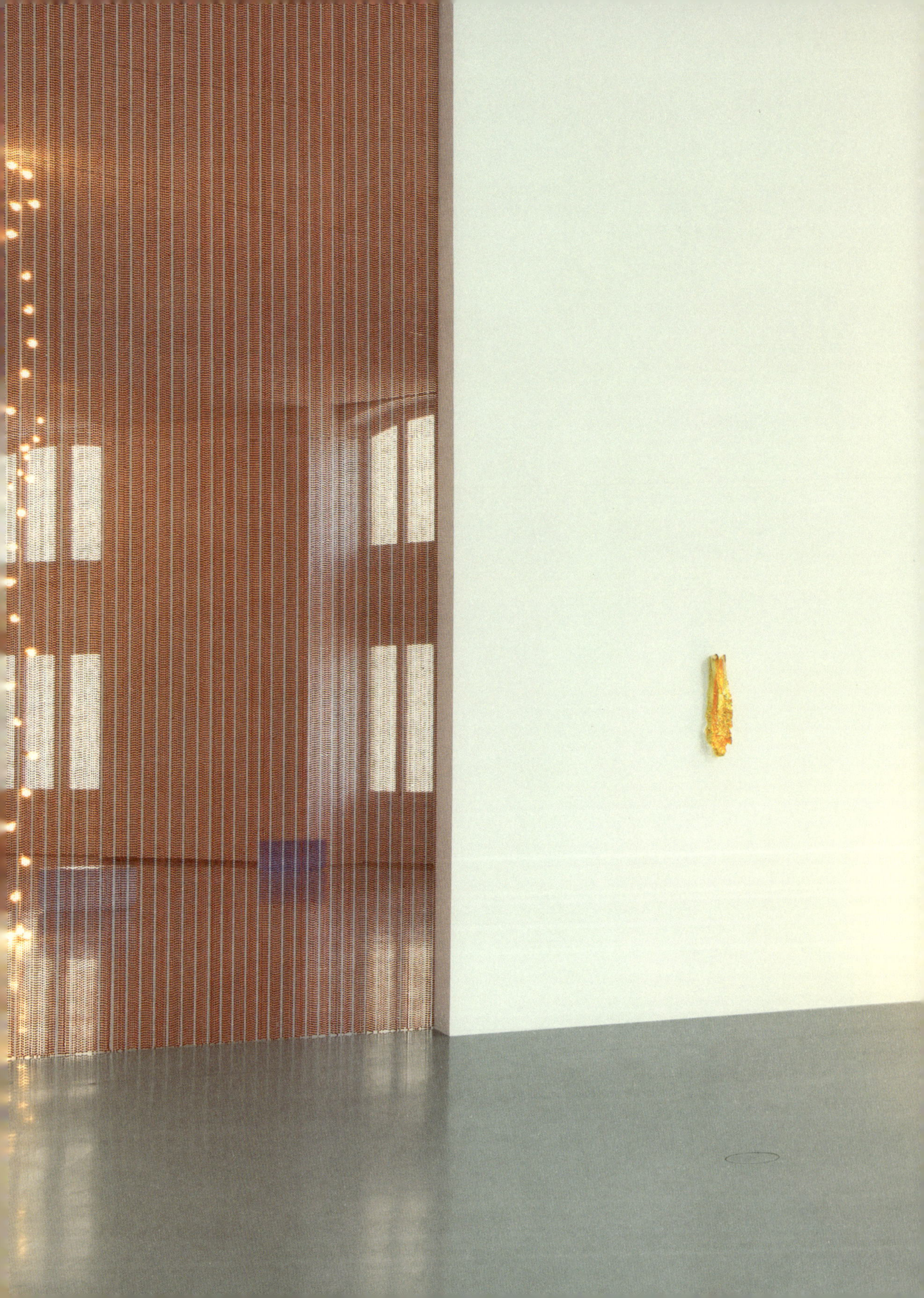

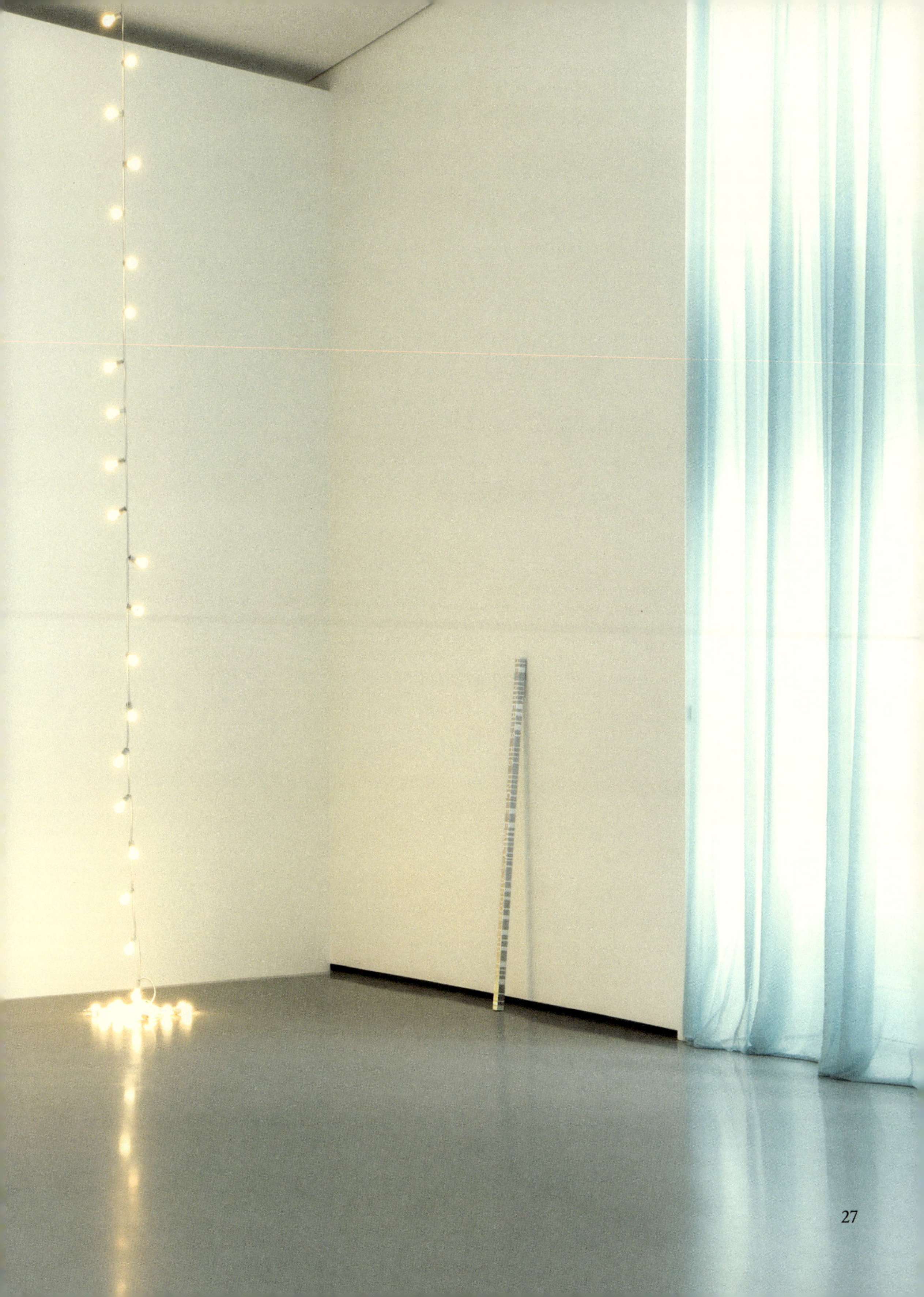

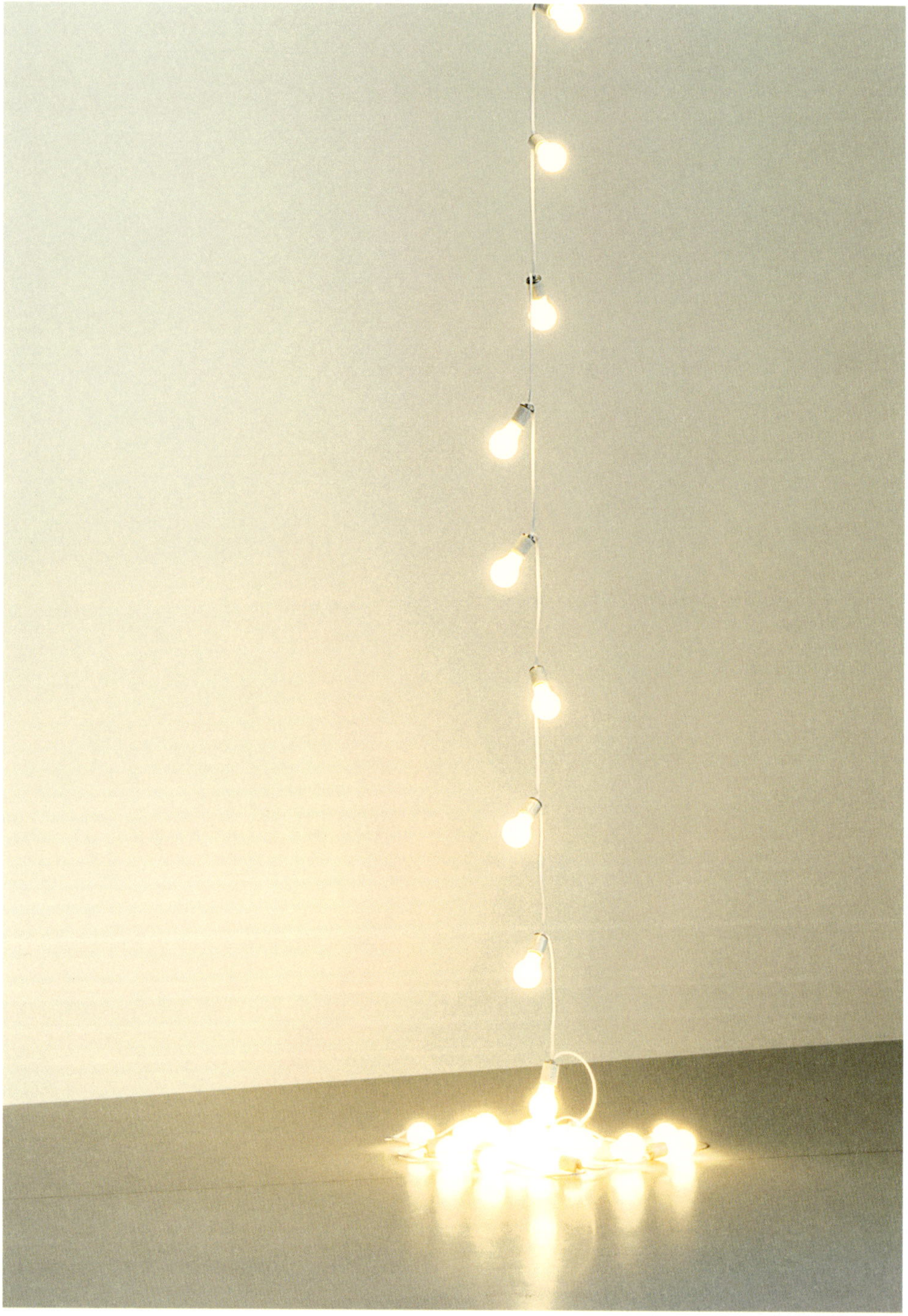

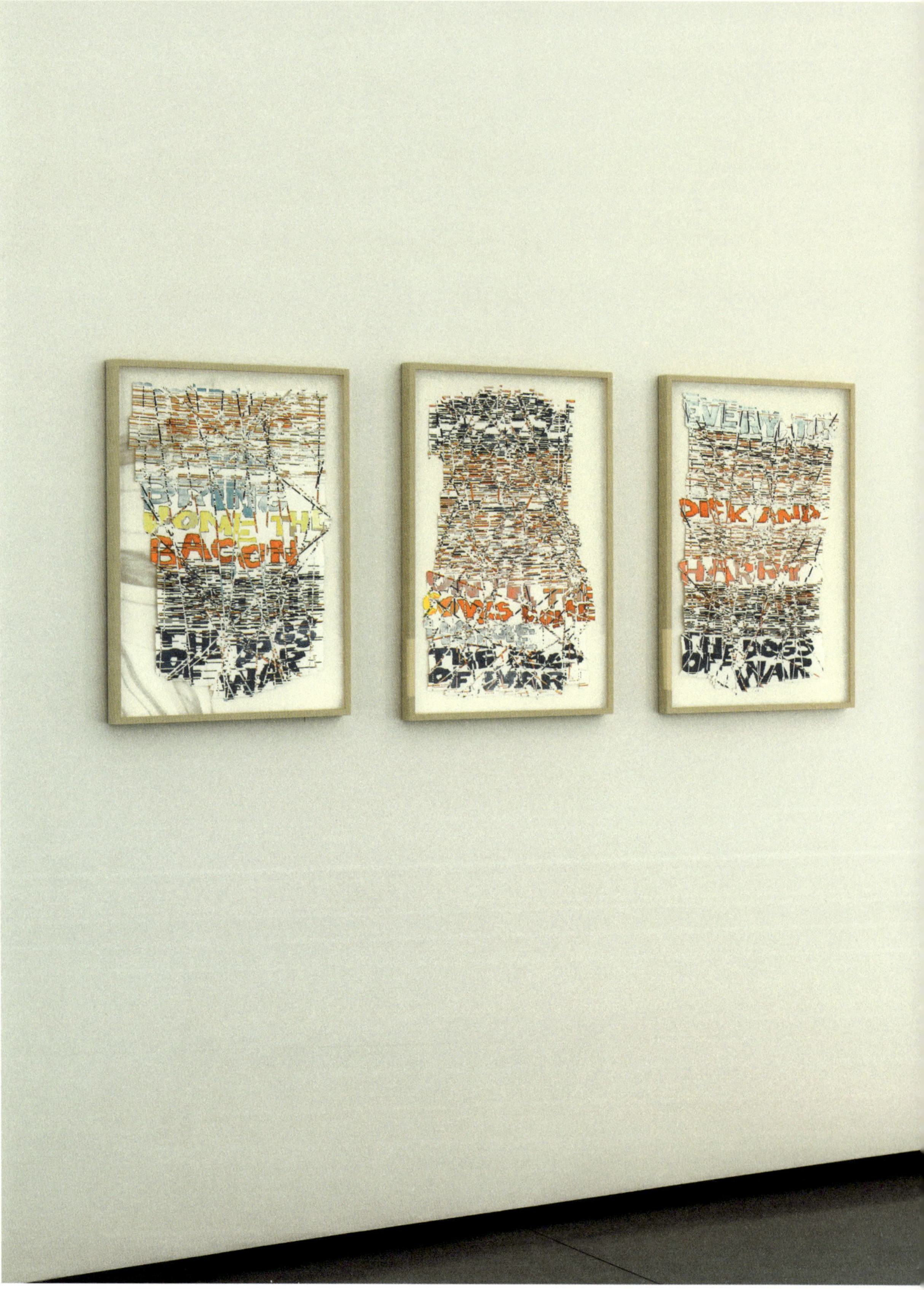
HOME THE
BACON
THE DOGS
OF WAR
OF WAR
DICK AND
THE DOGS
OF WAR

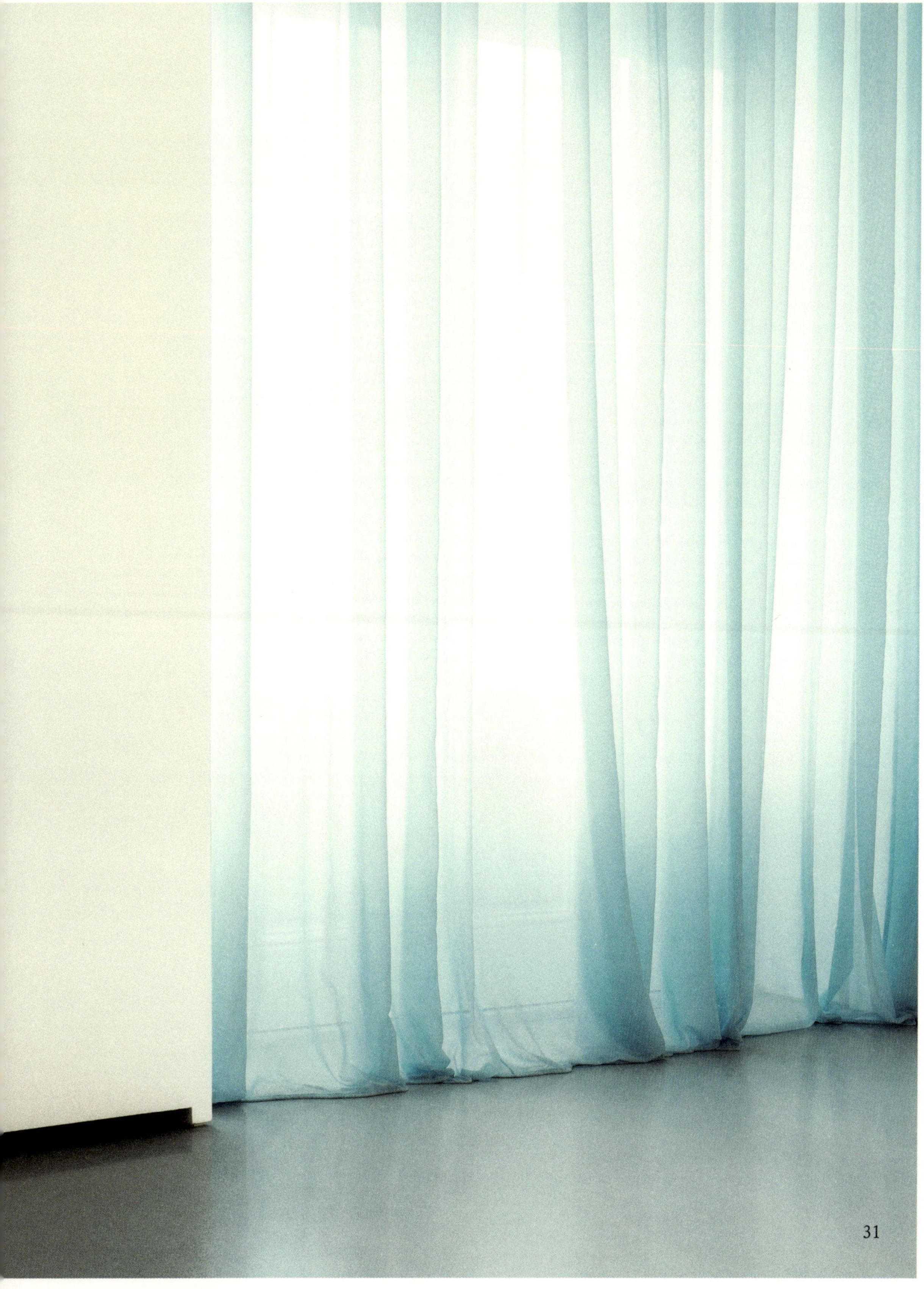

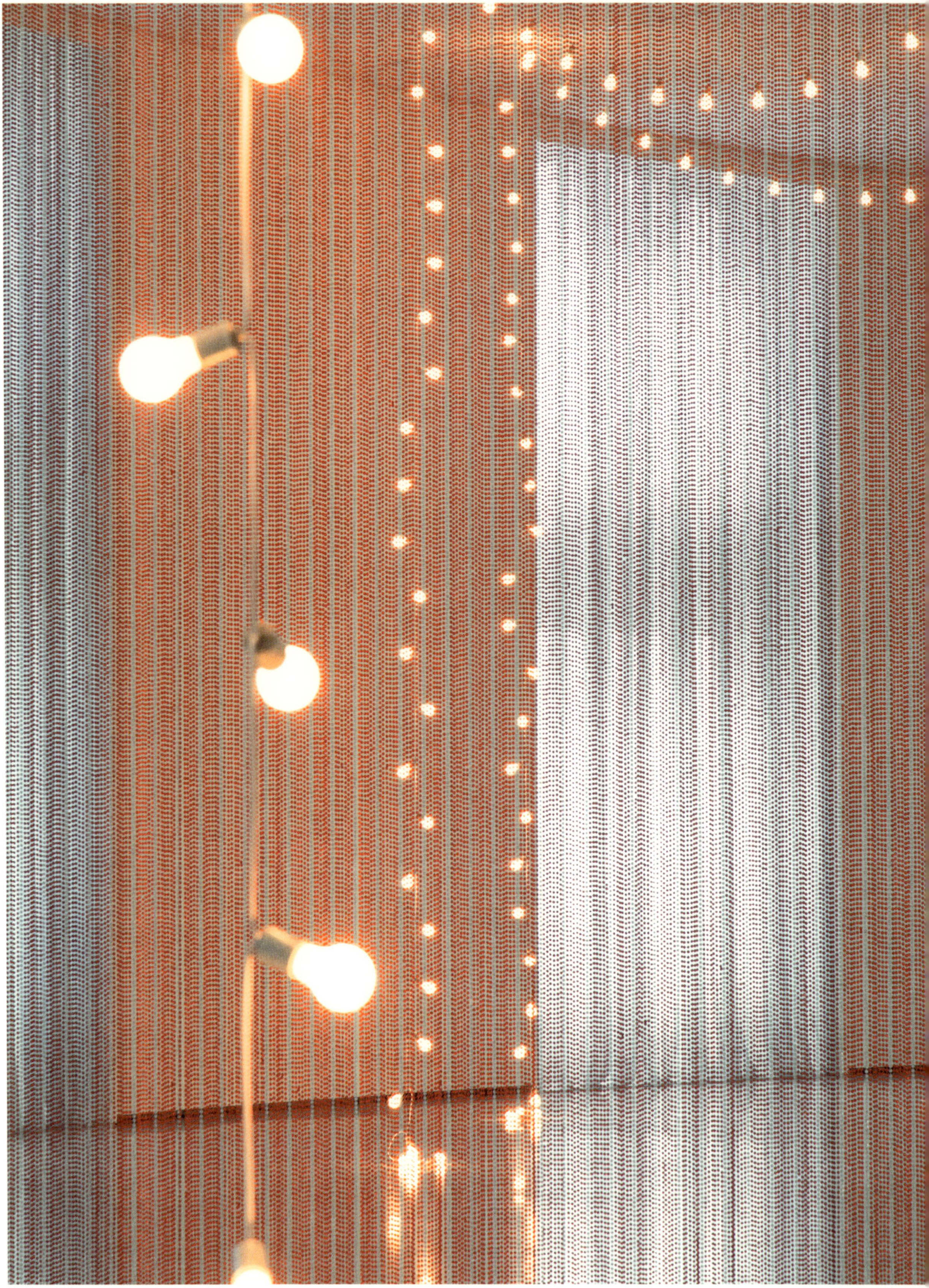

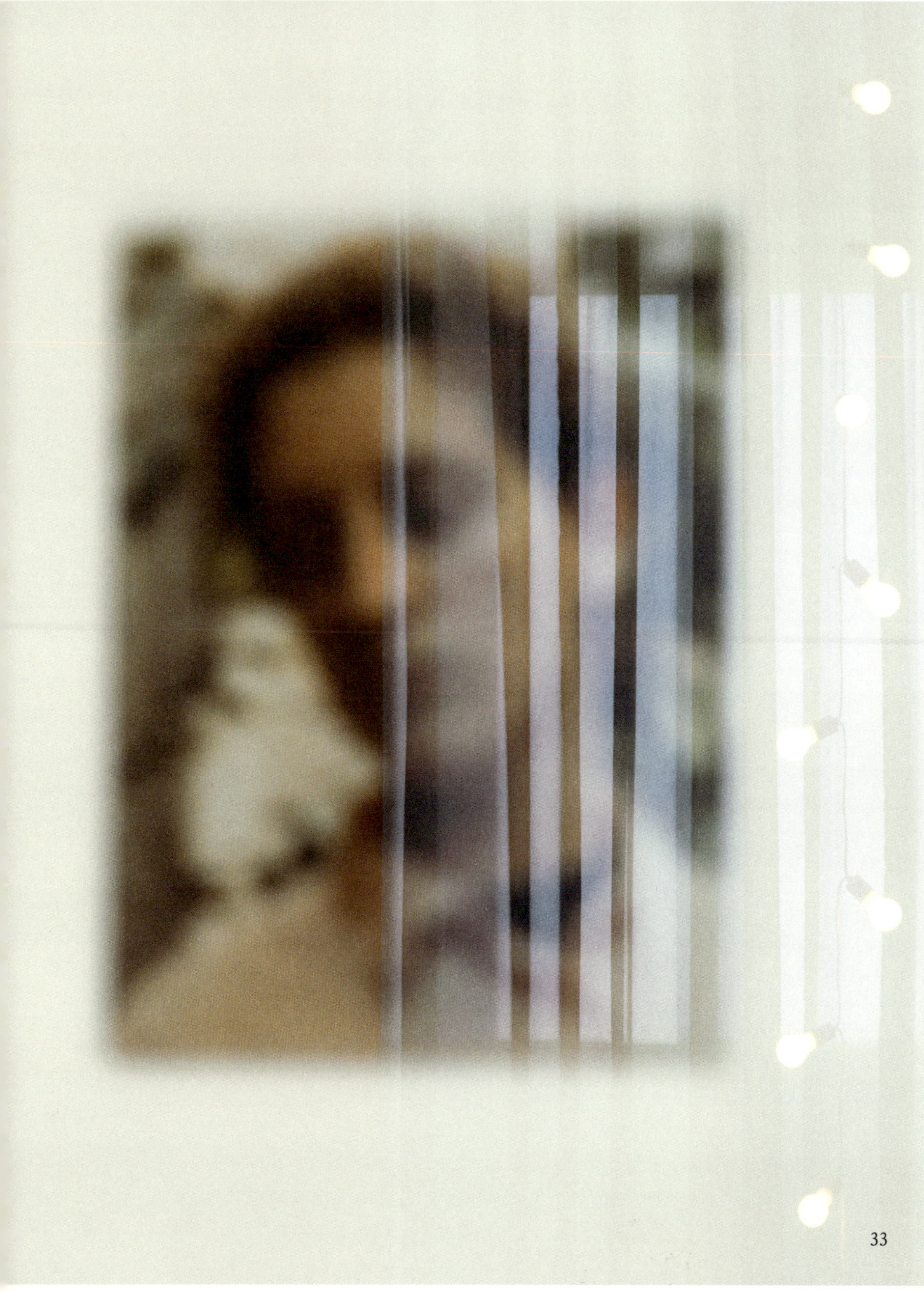

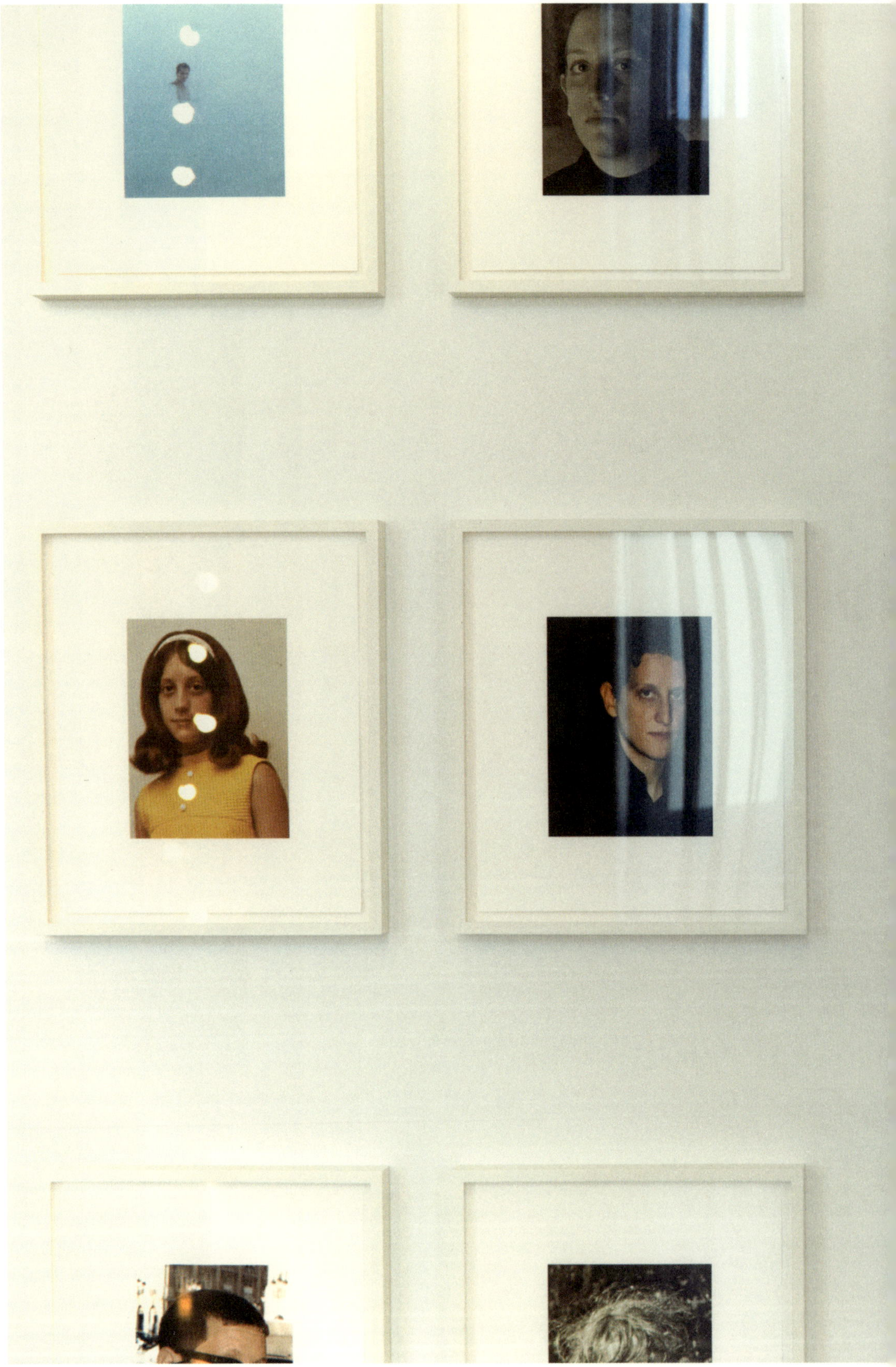

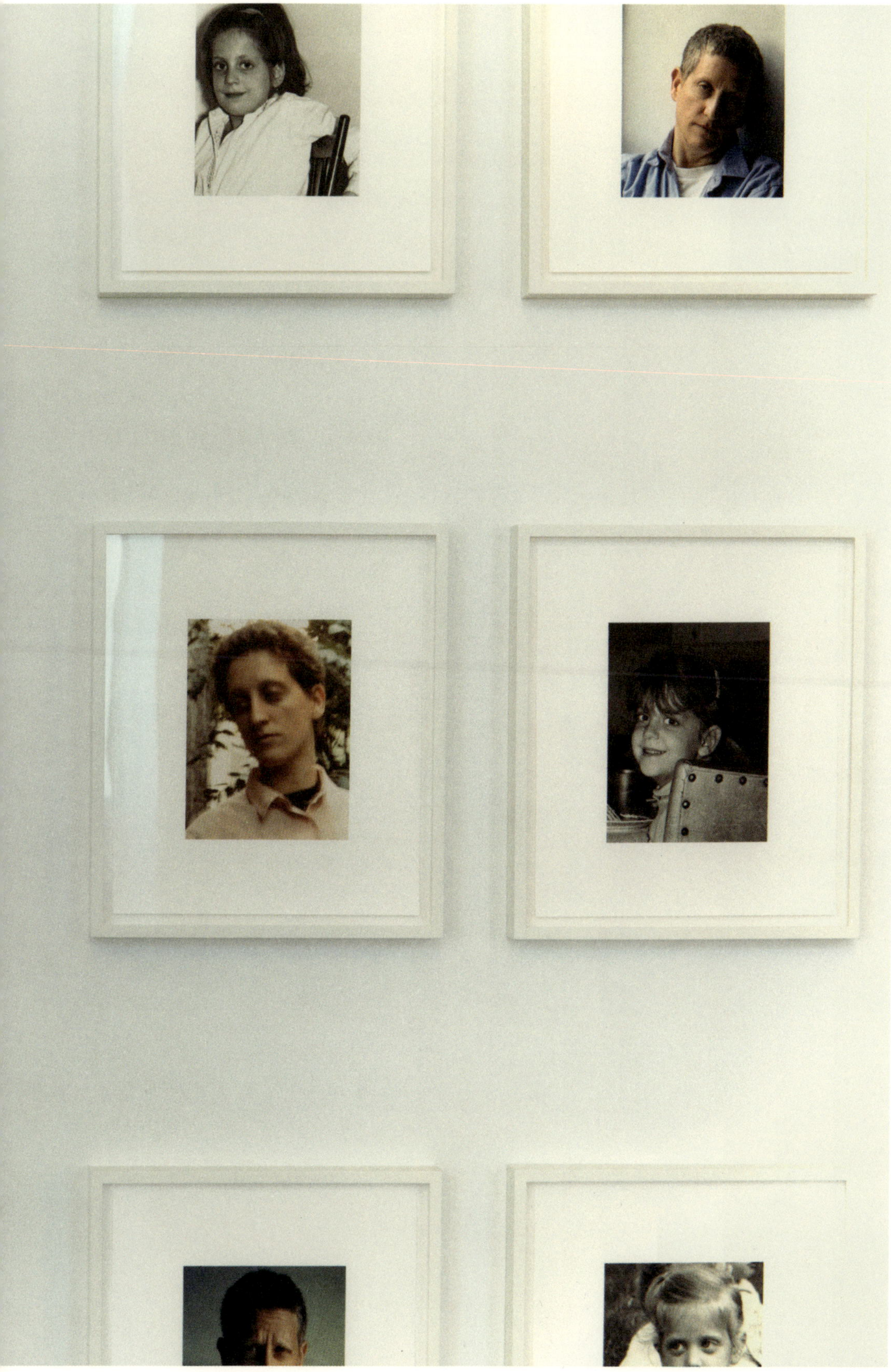

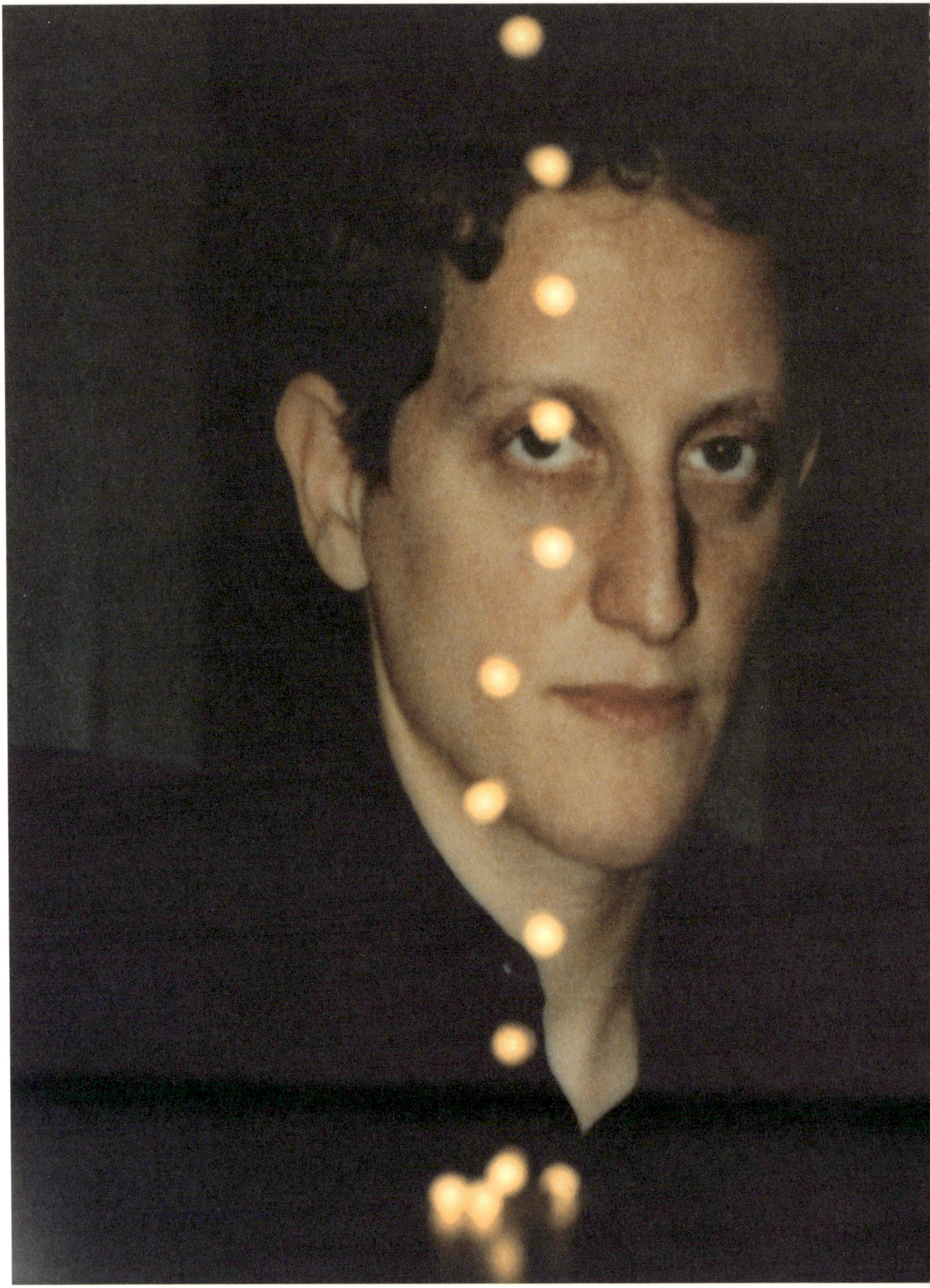

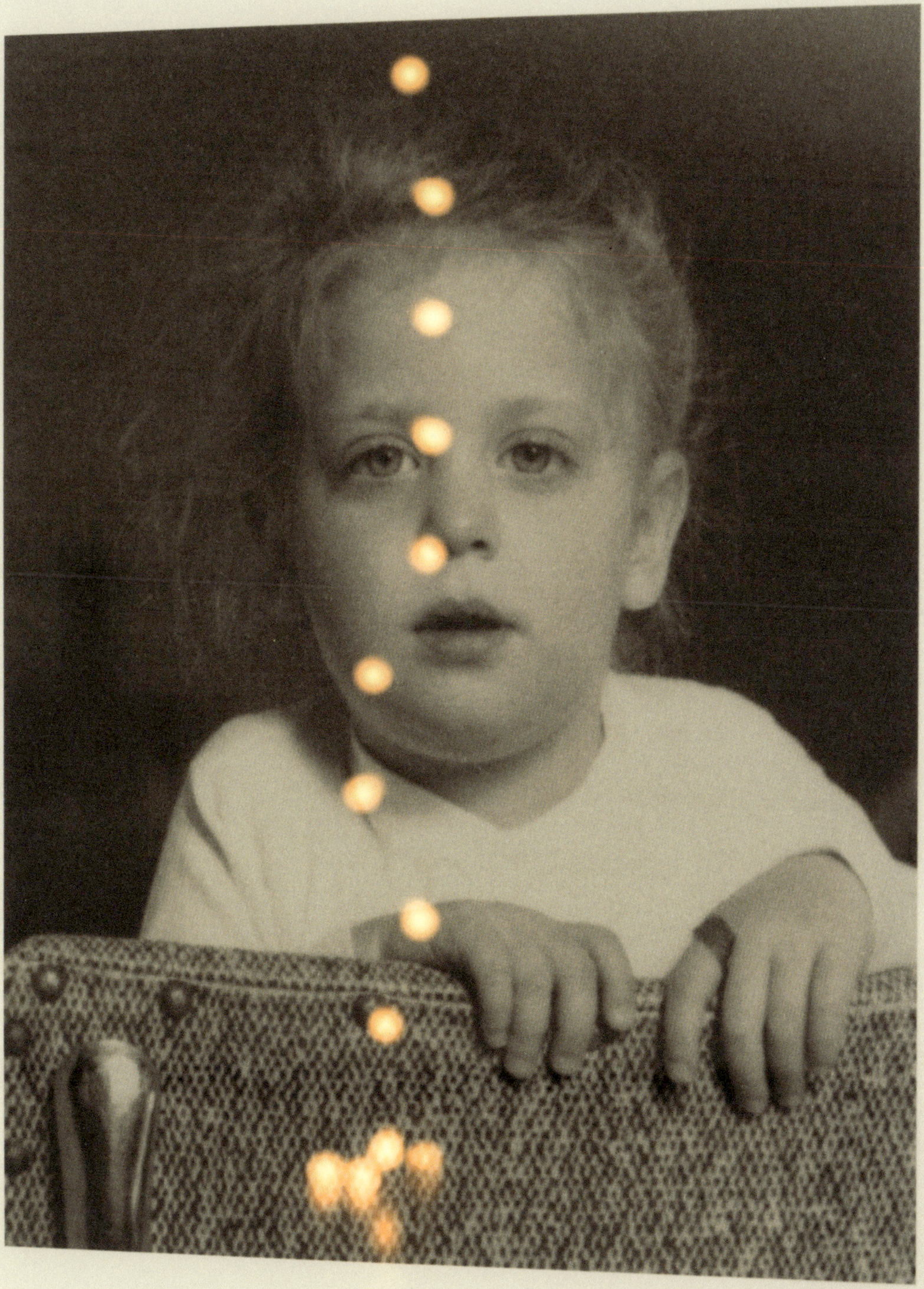

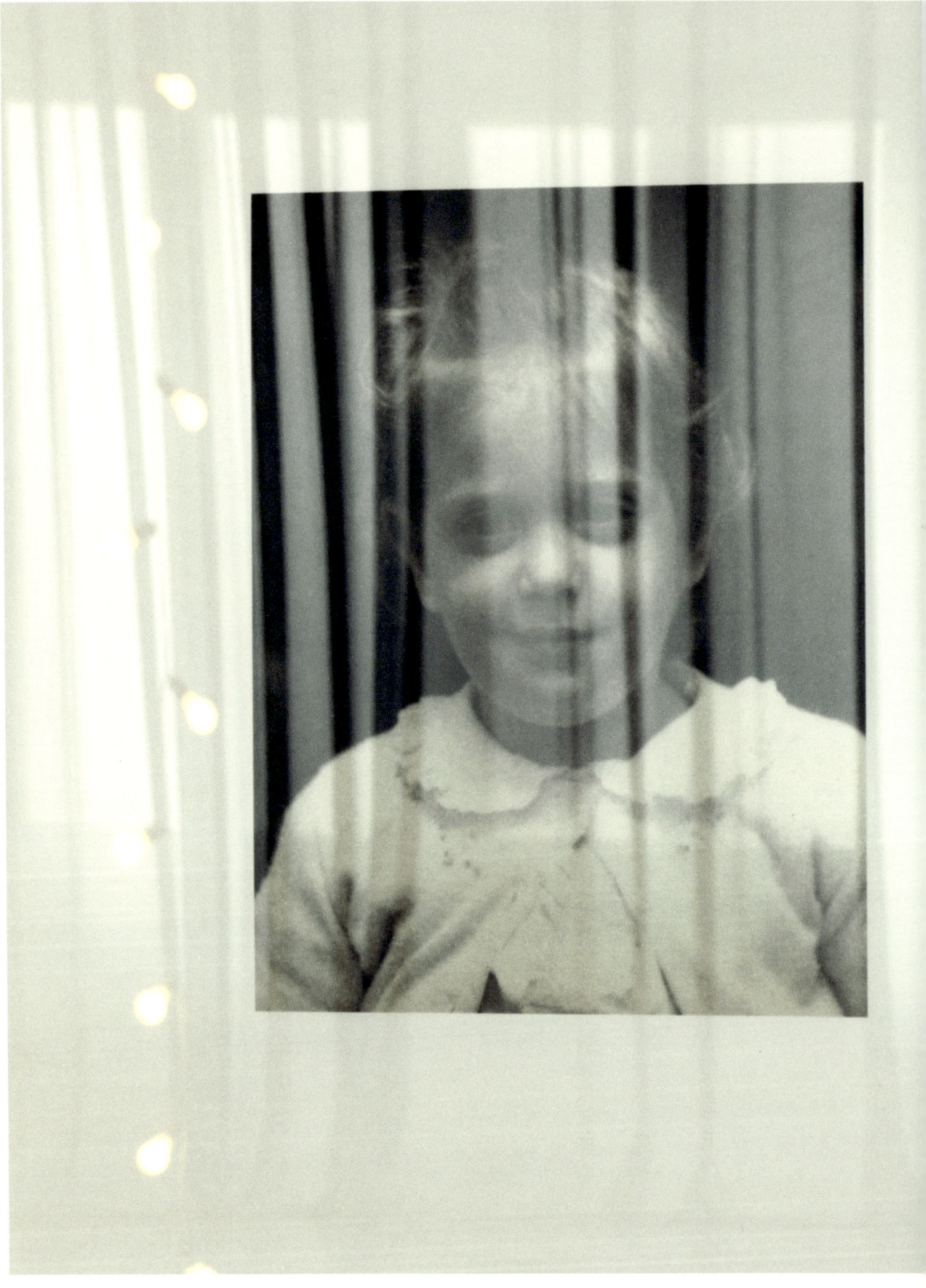

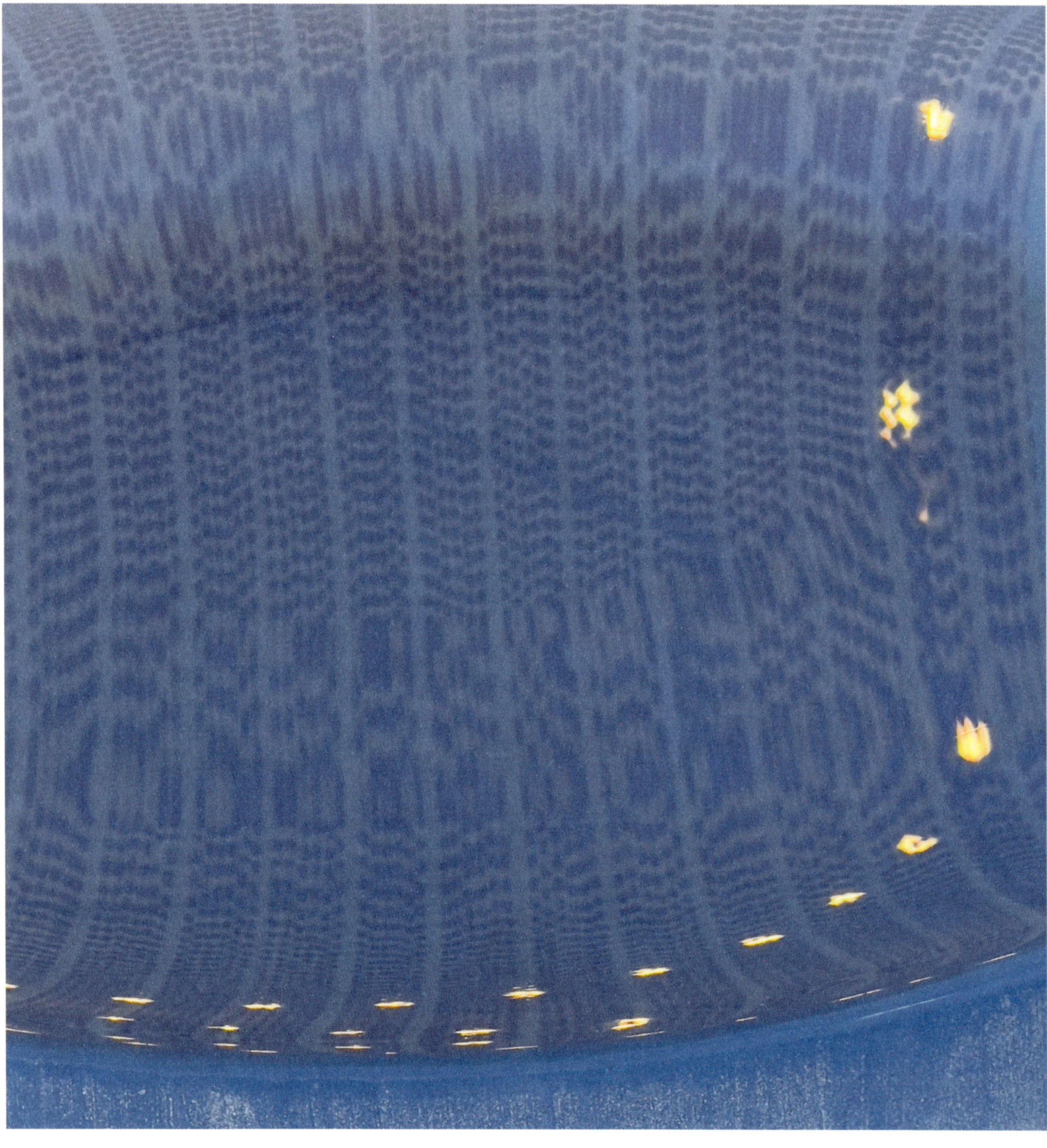

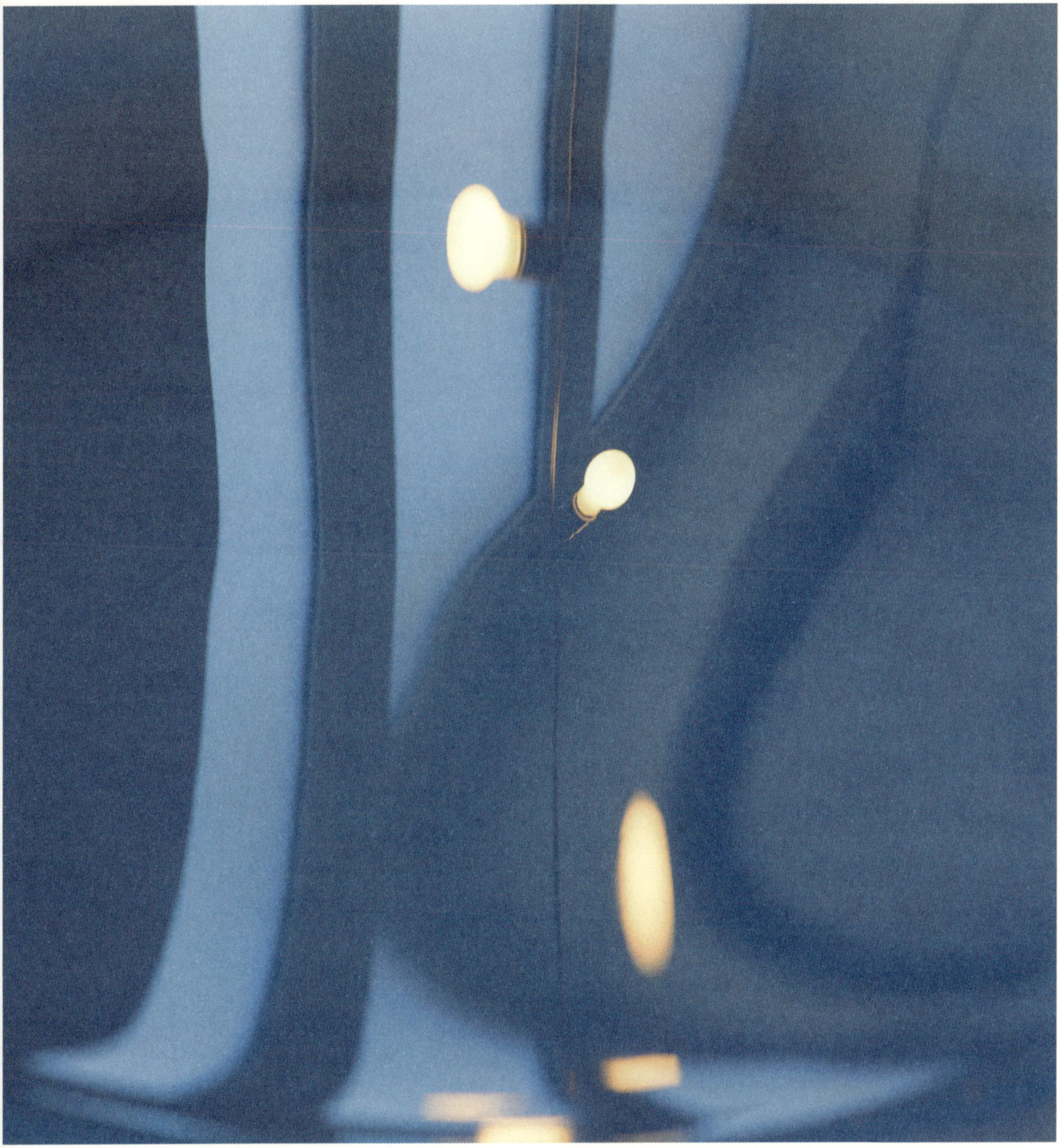

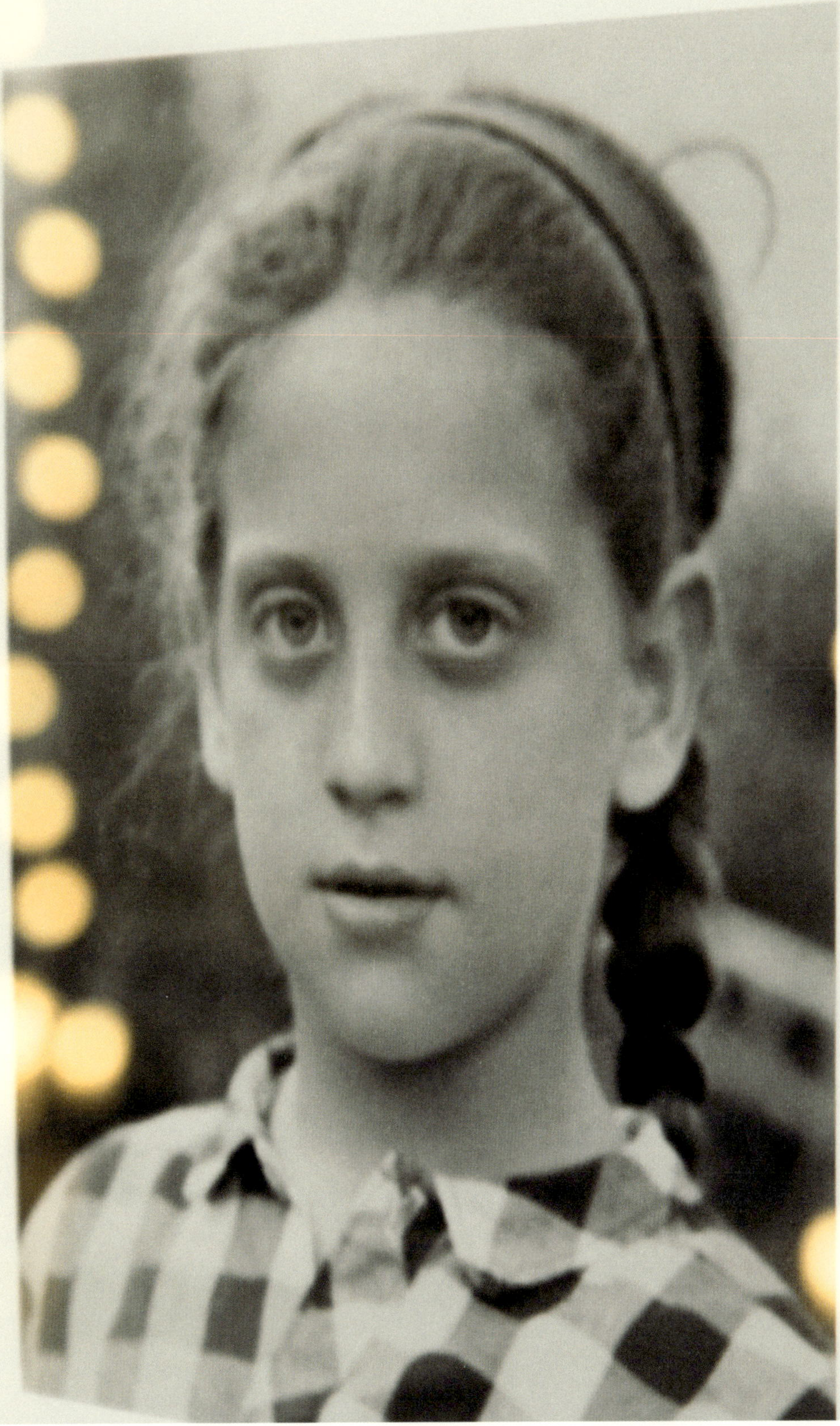

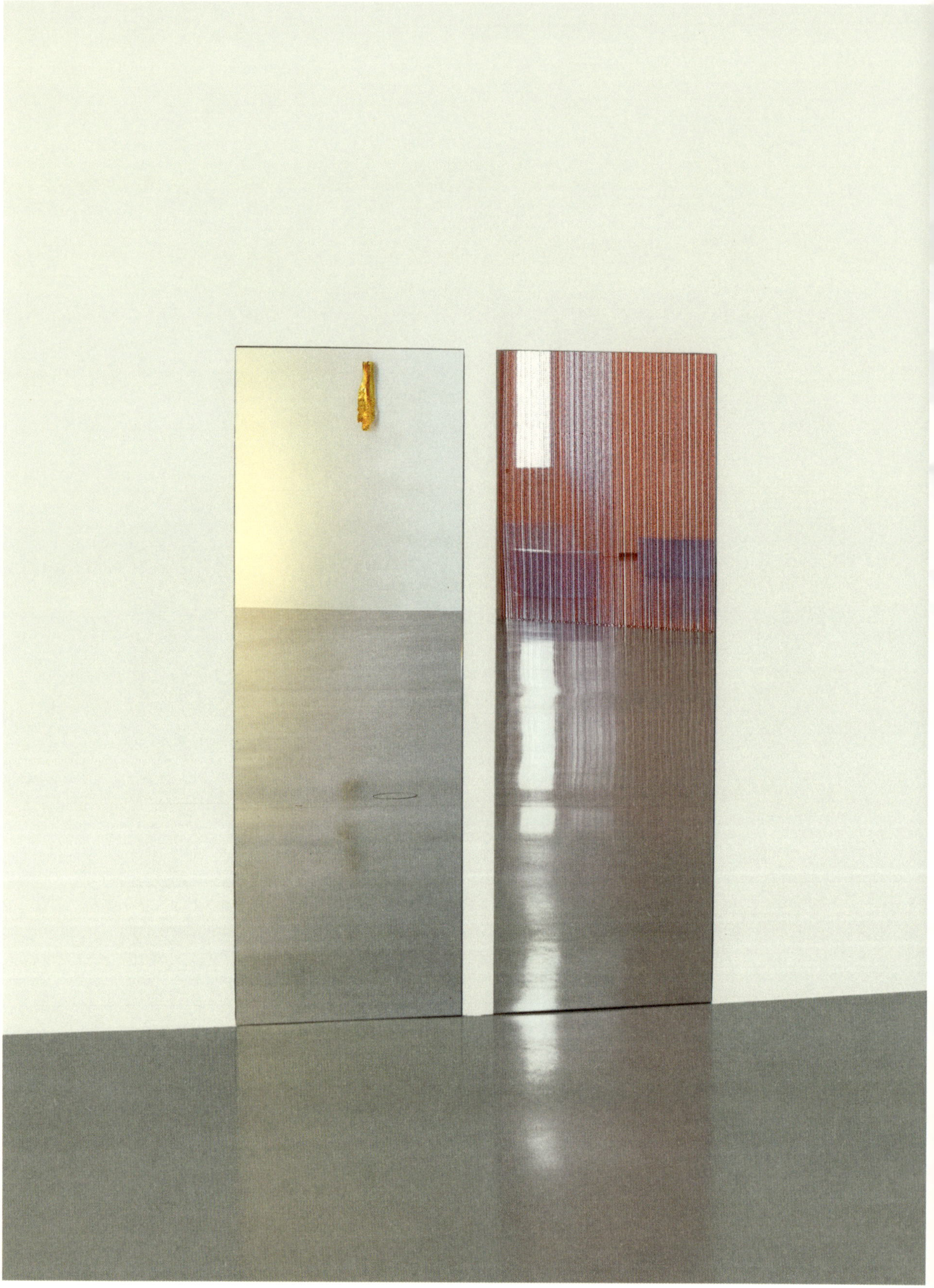

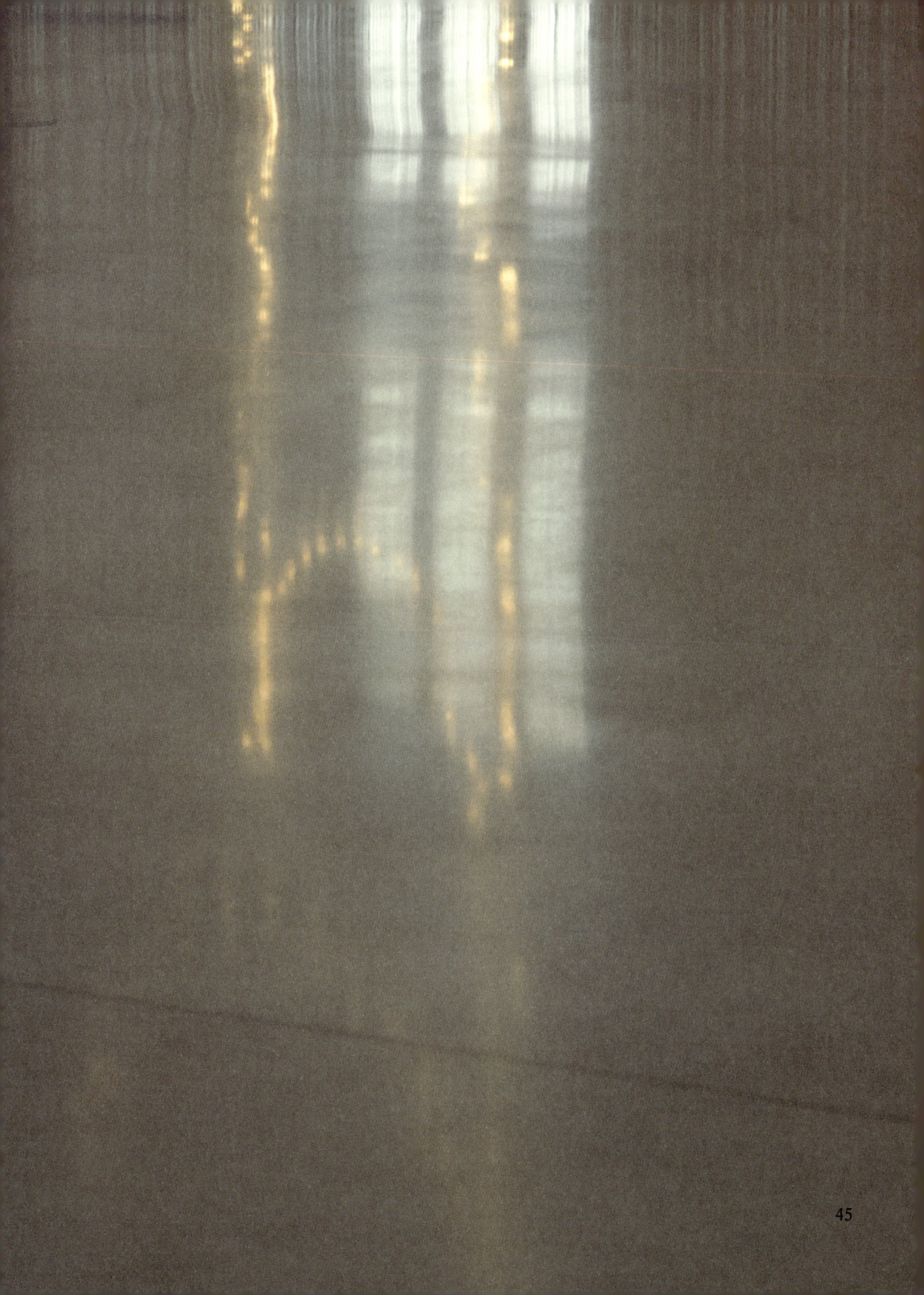

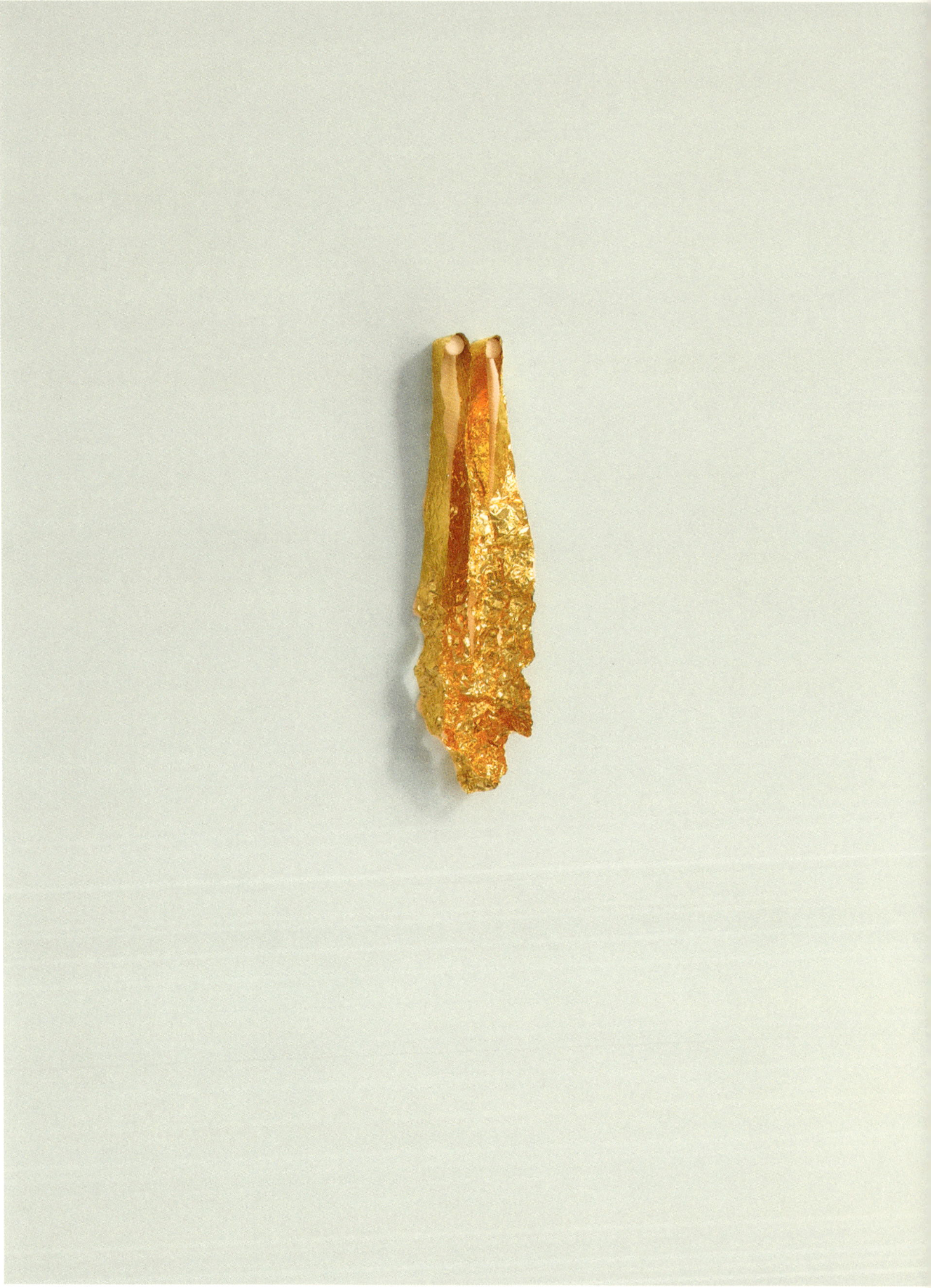

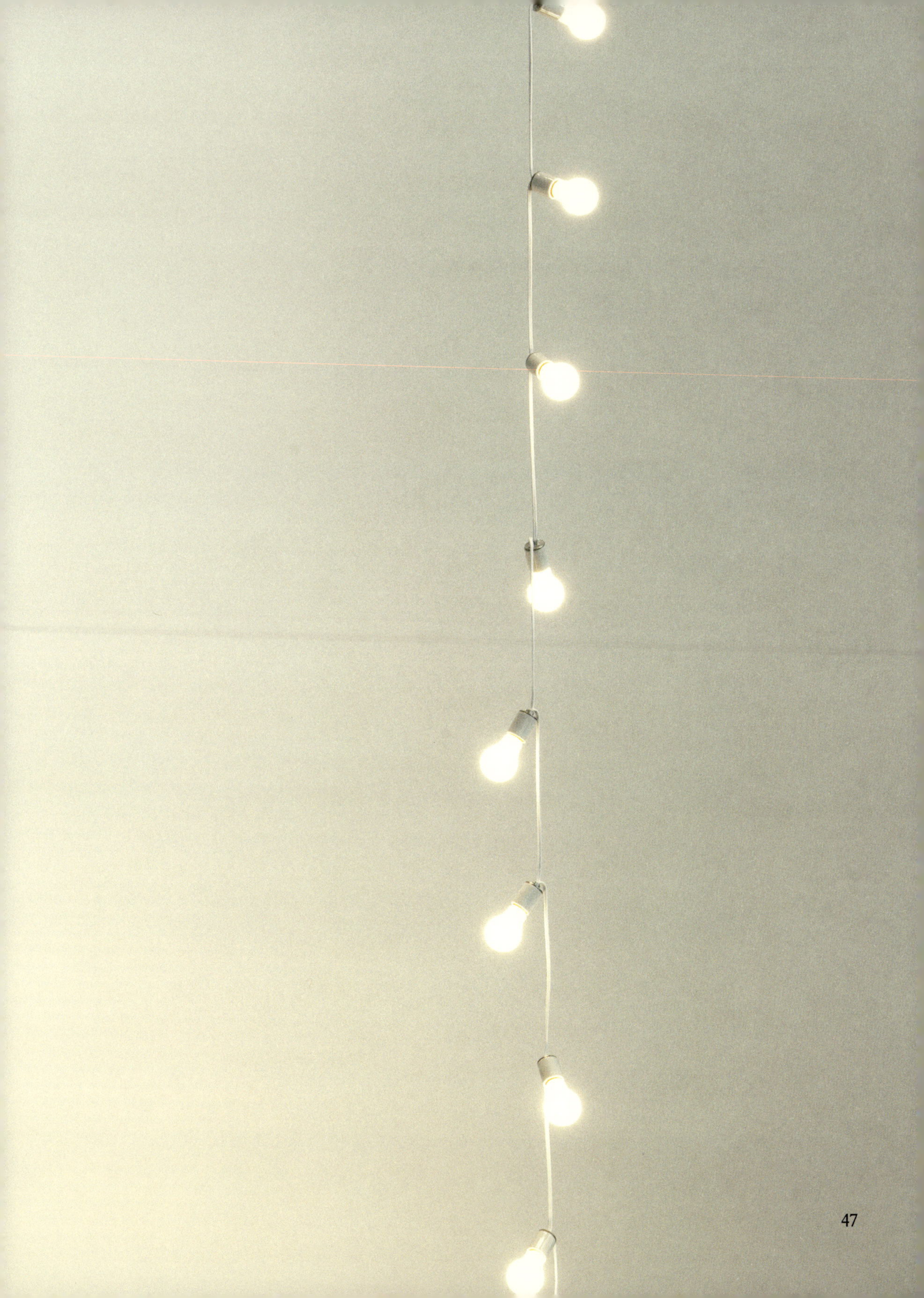

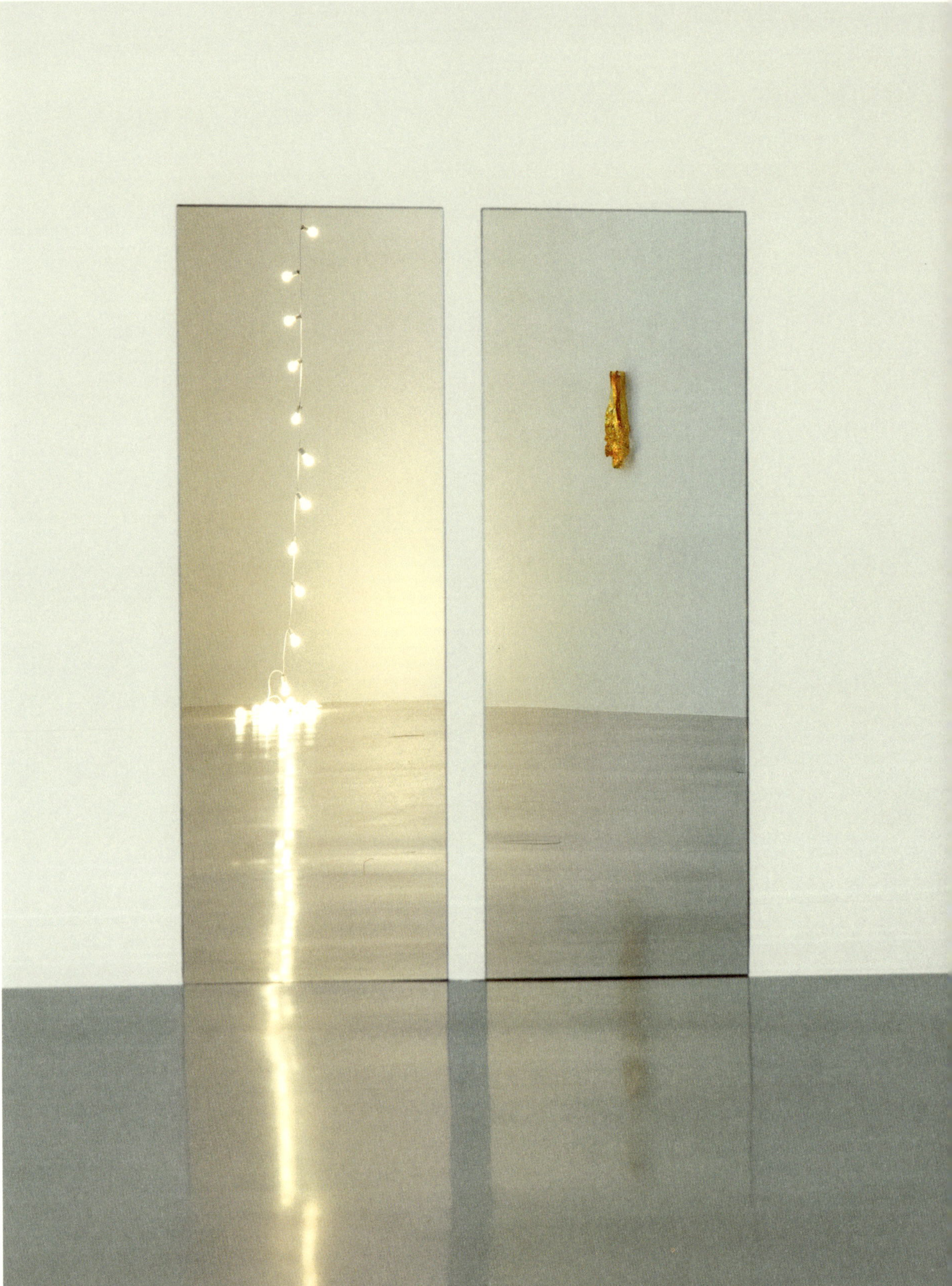

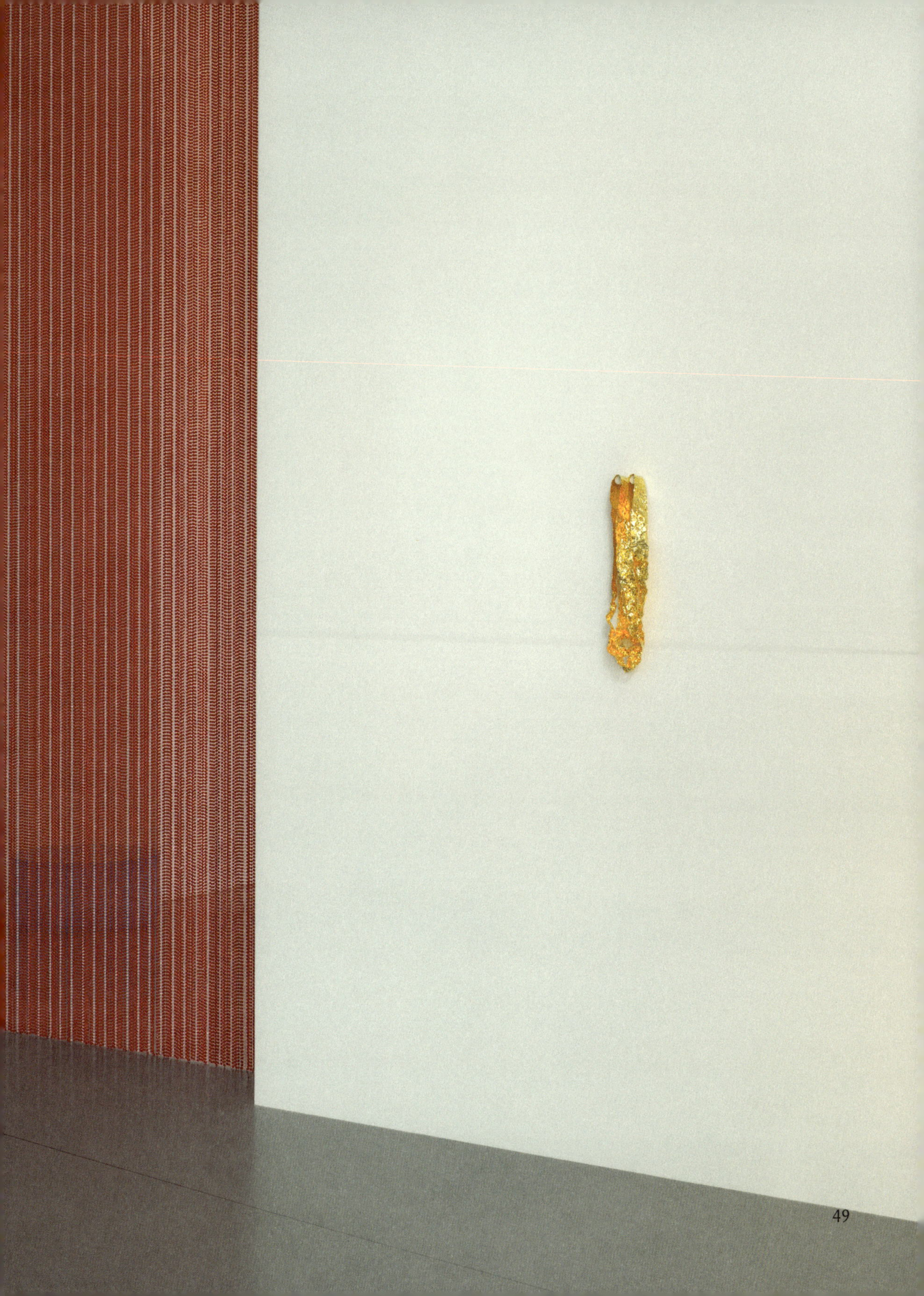

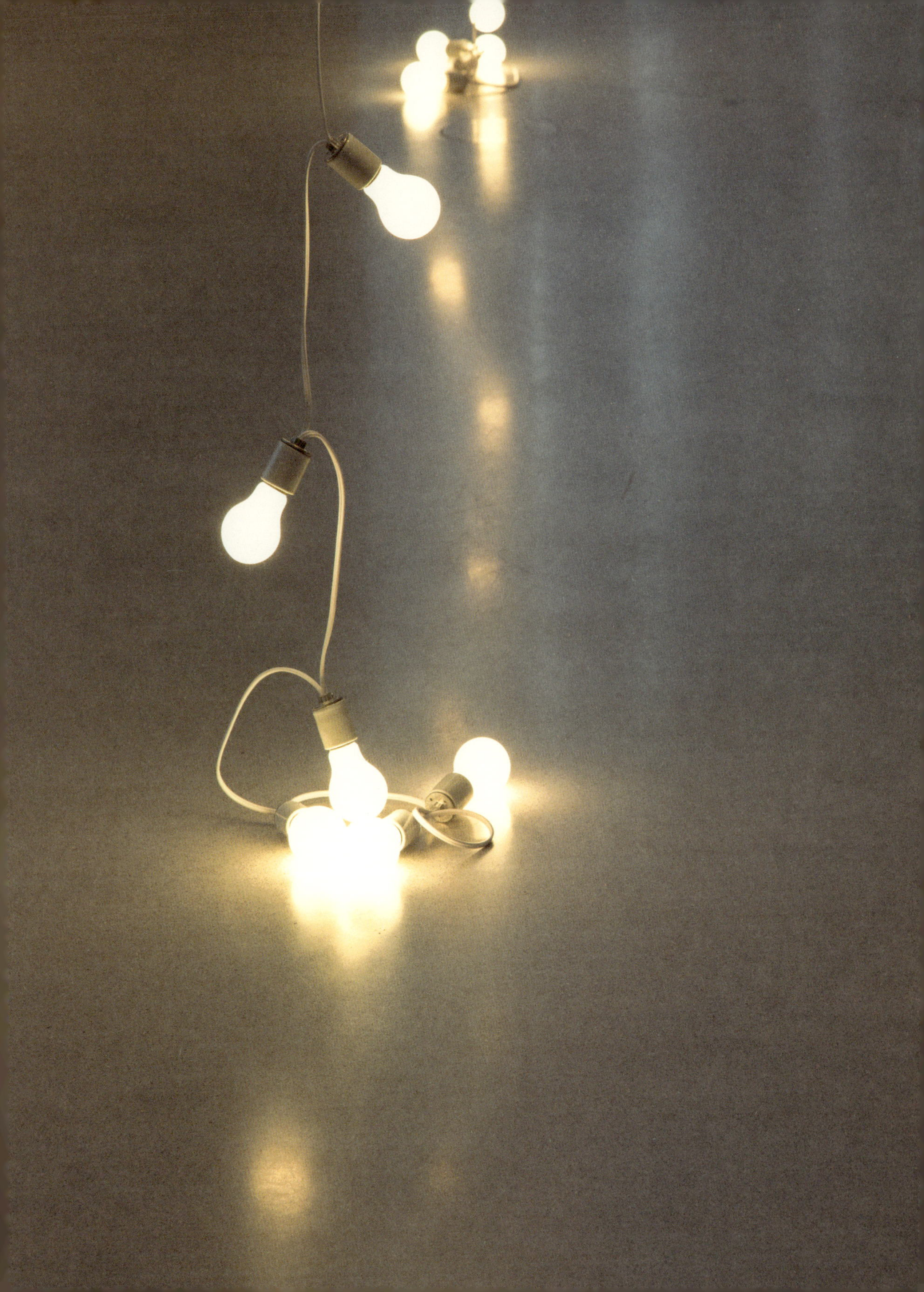

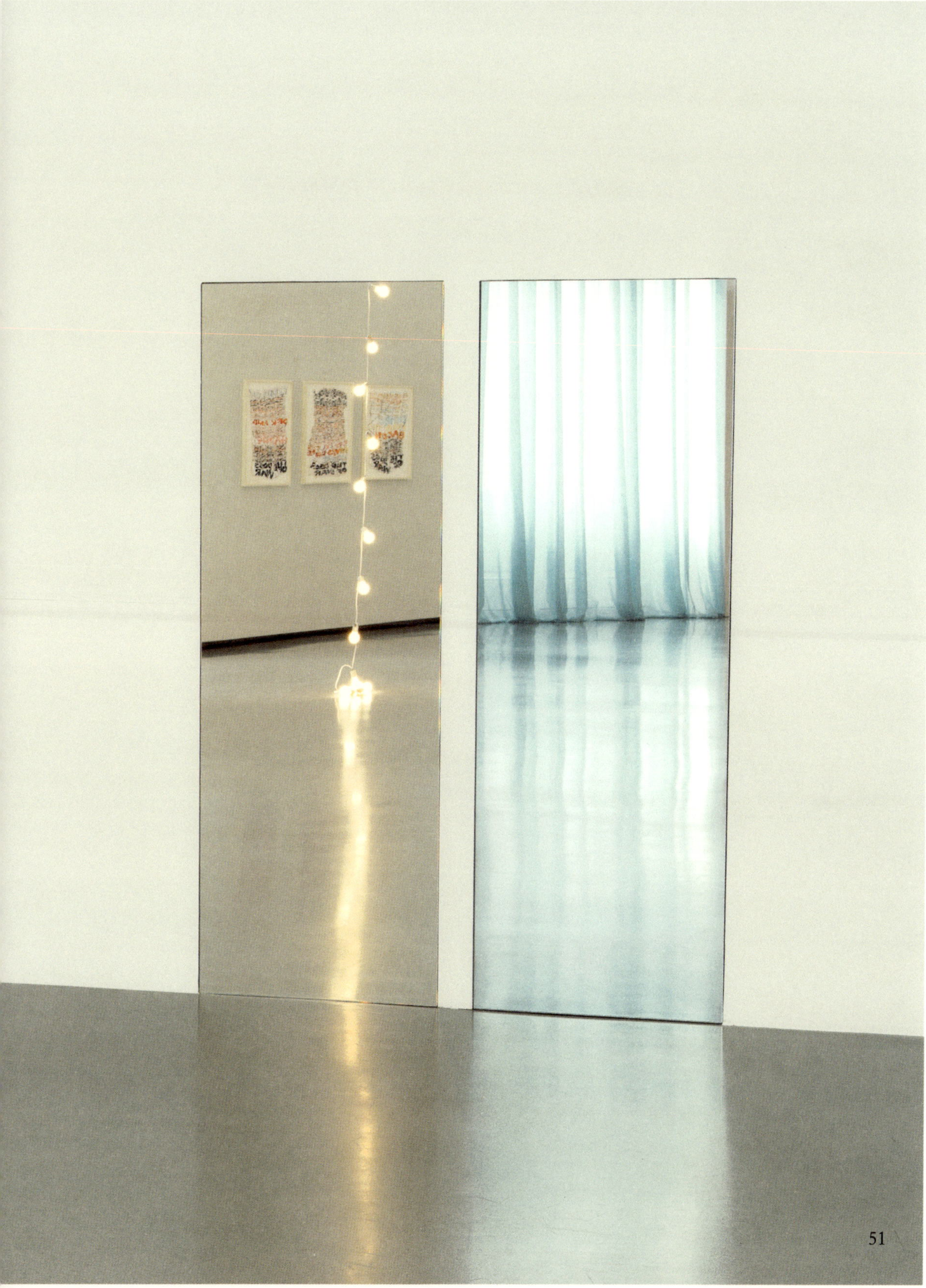

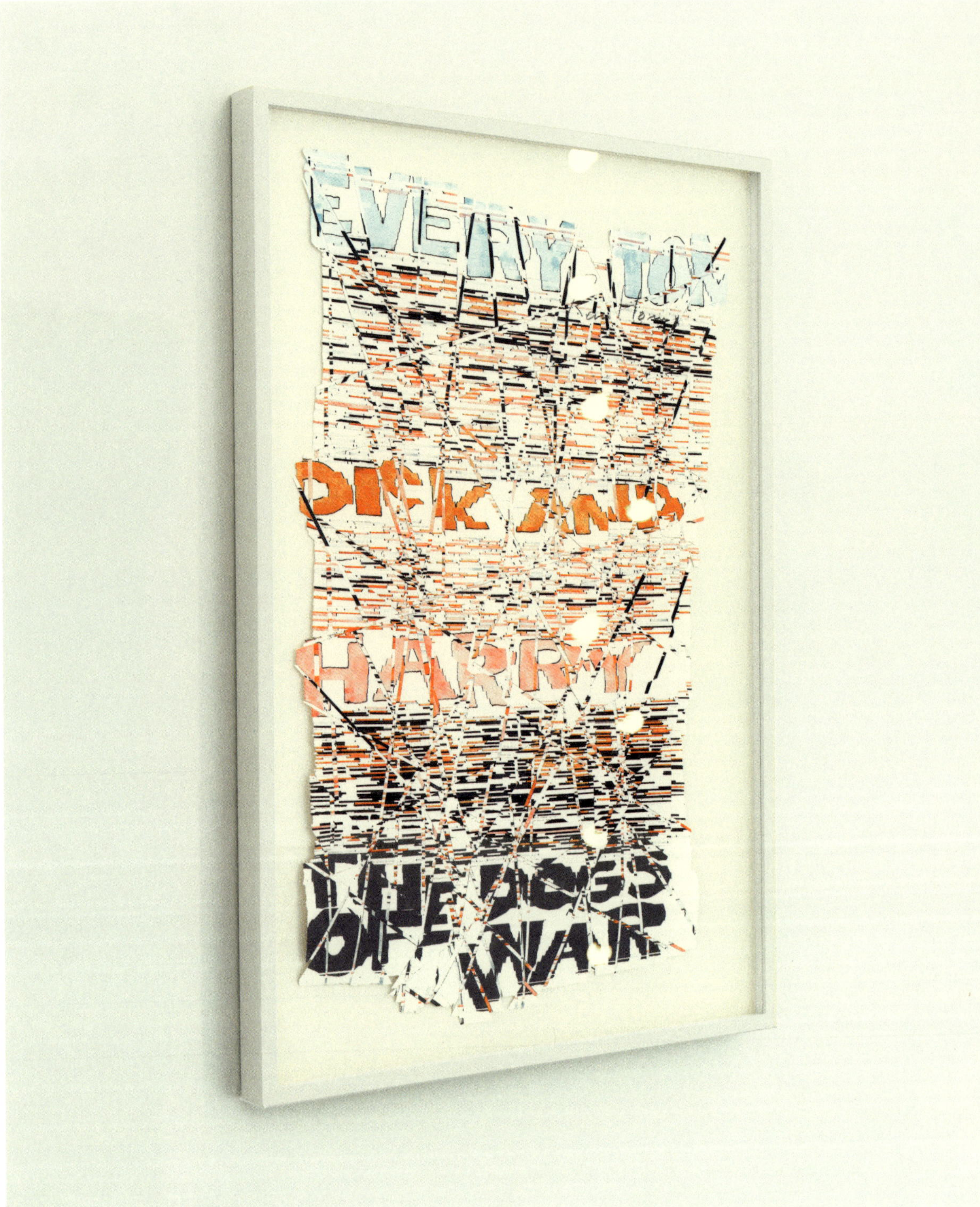
EVERY TOM
DICK AND
HARRY
THE DOGS
OF WAR

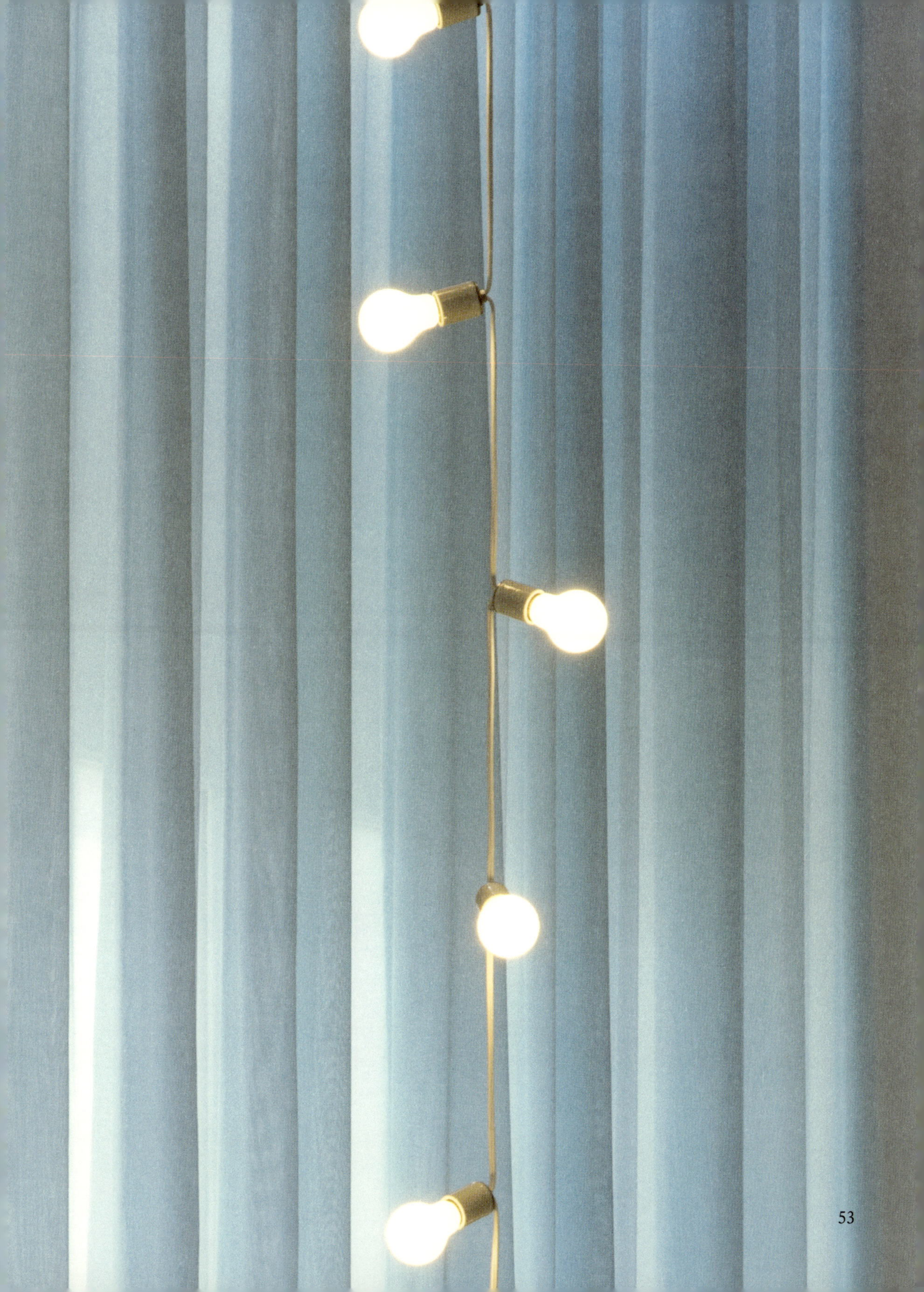

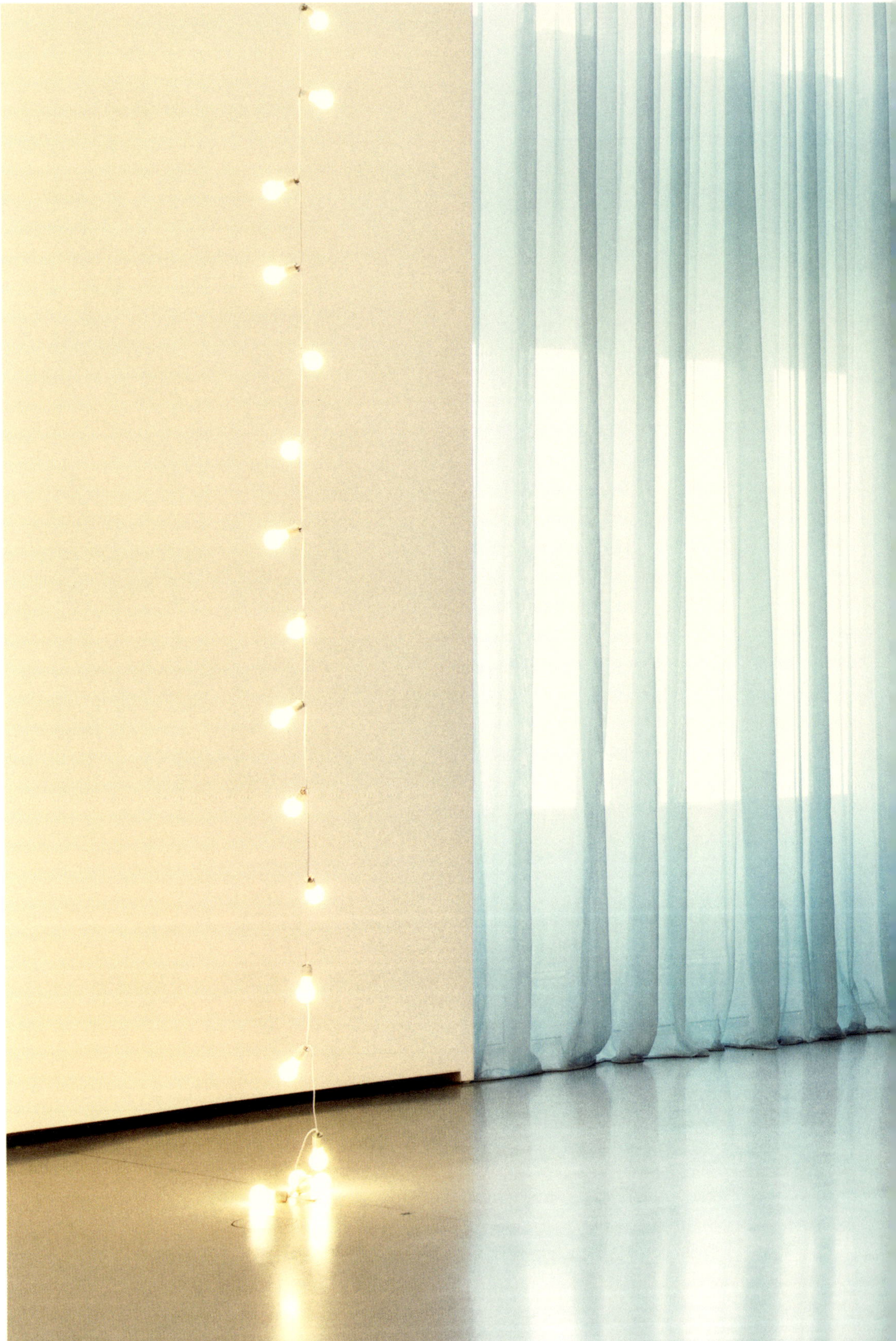

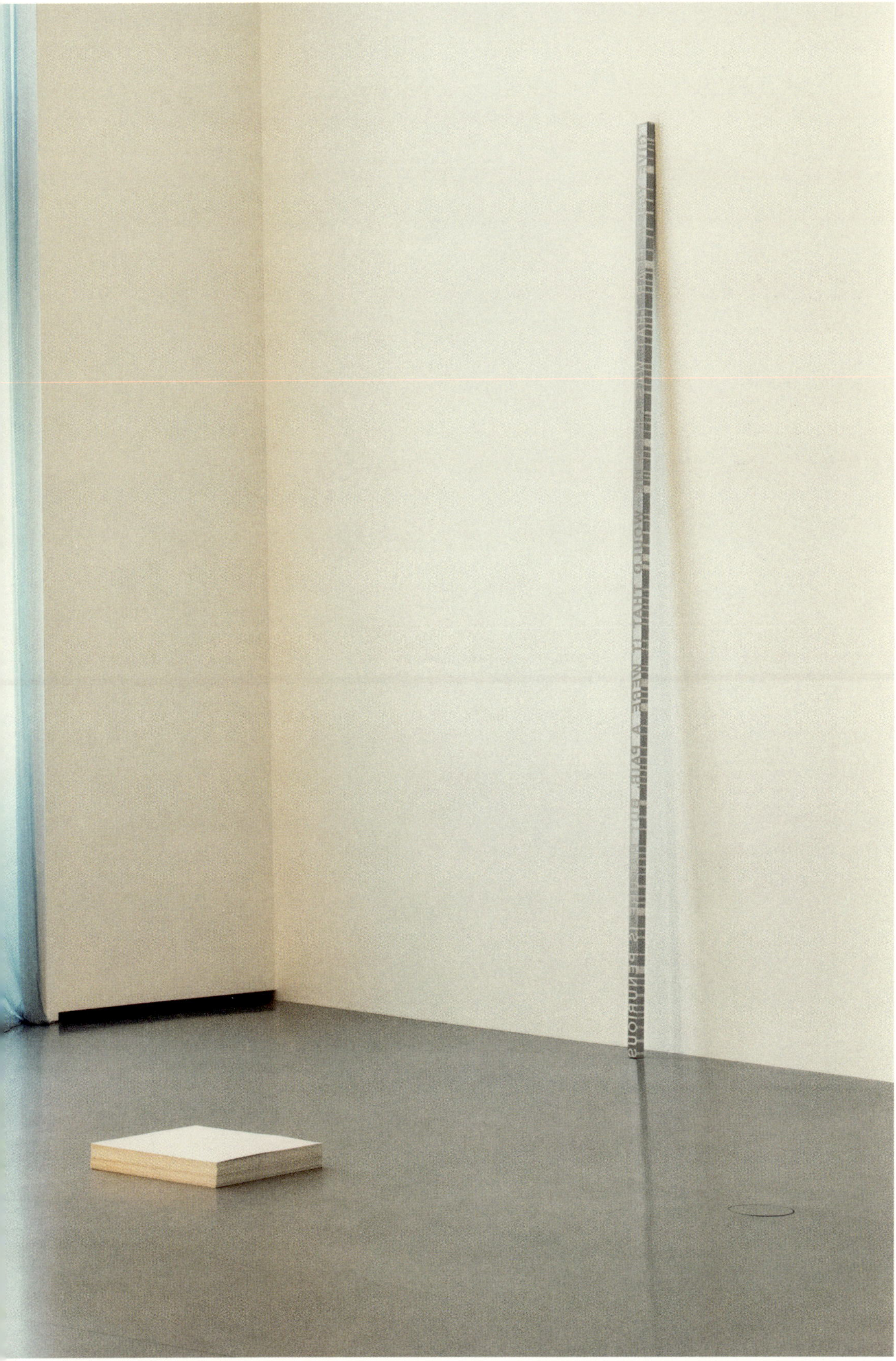

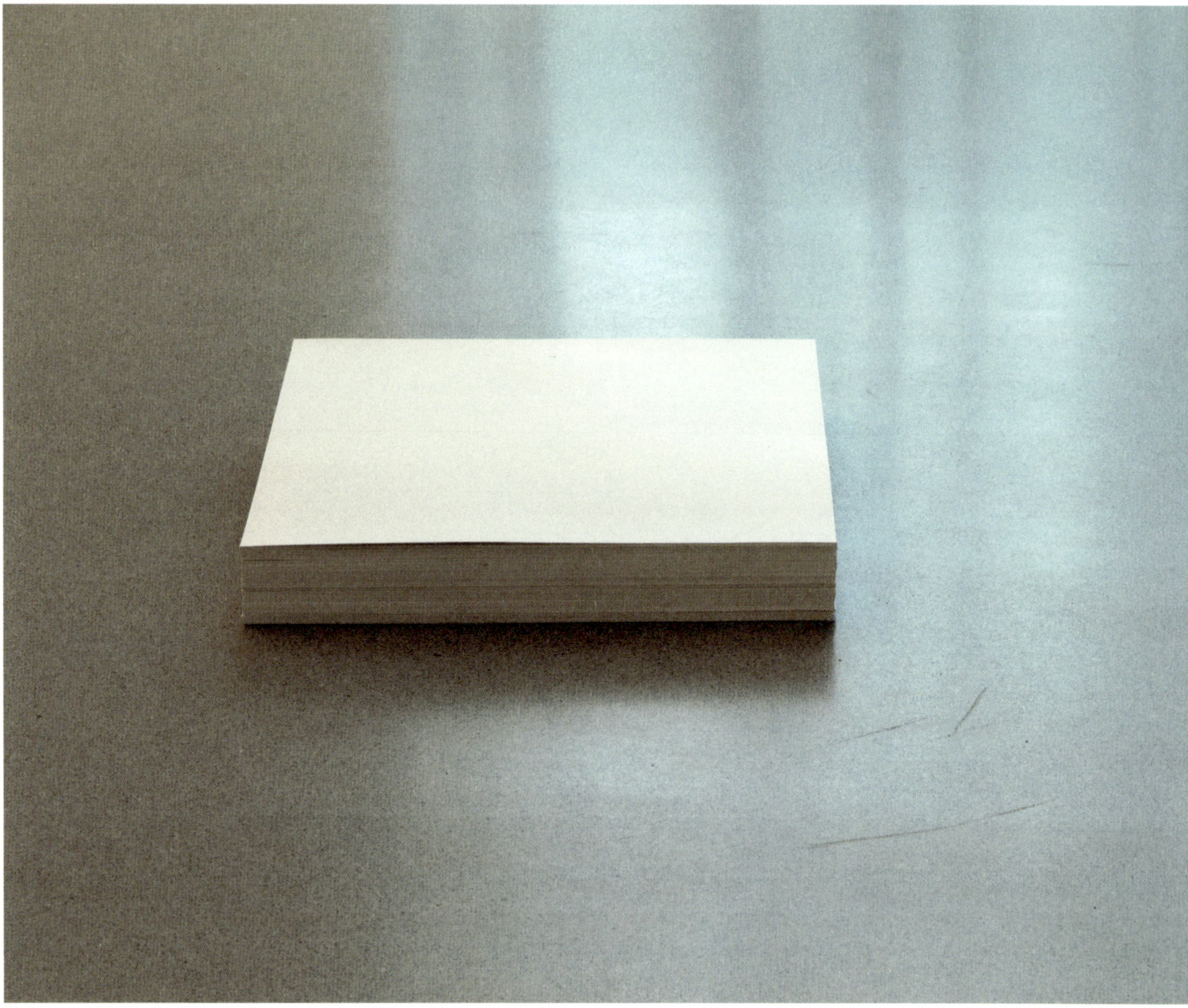

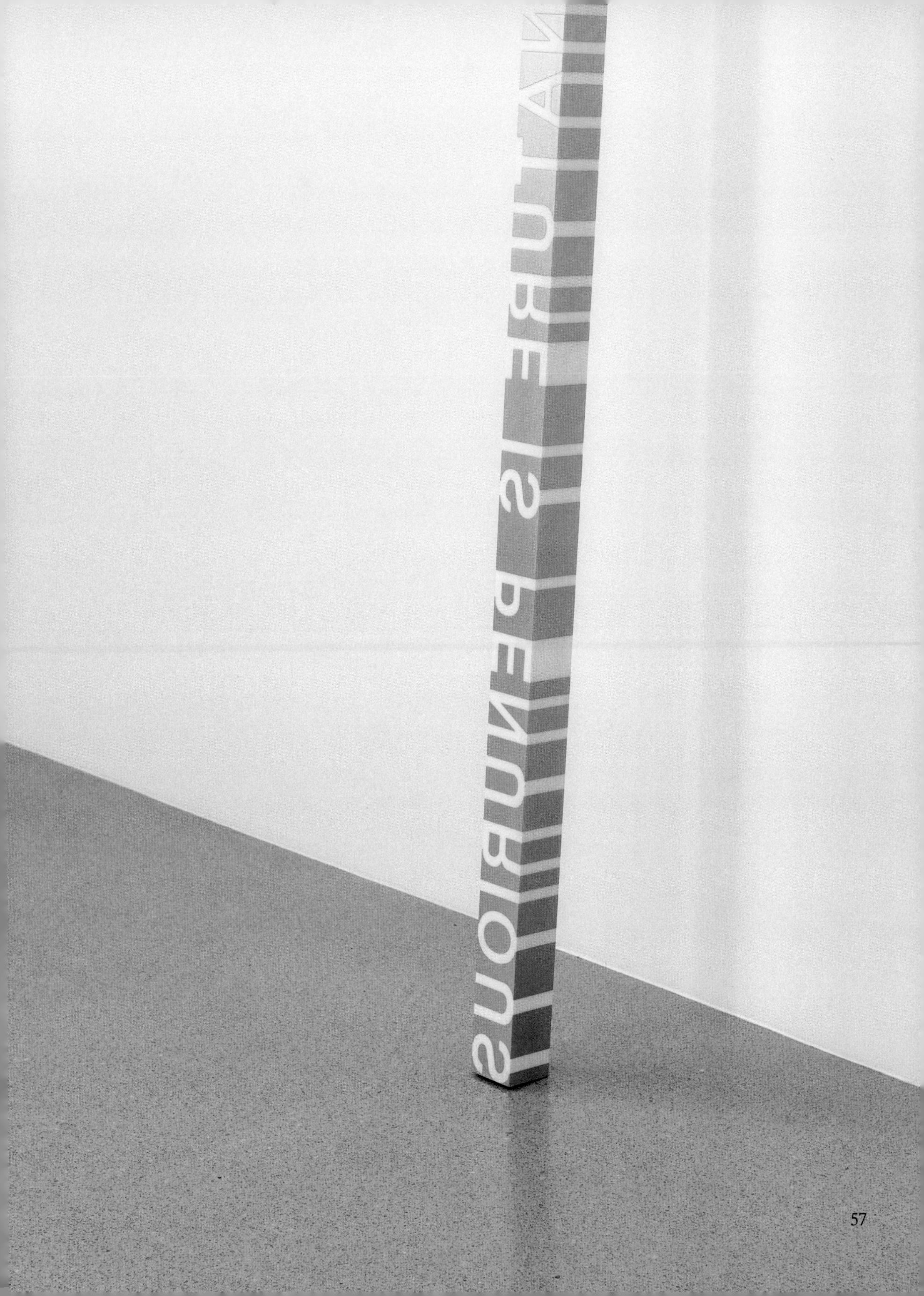

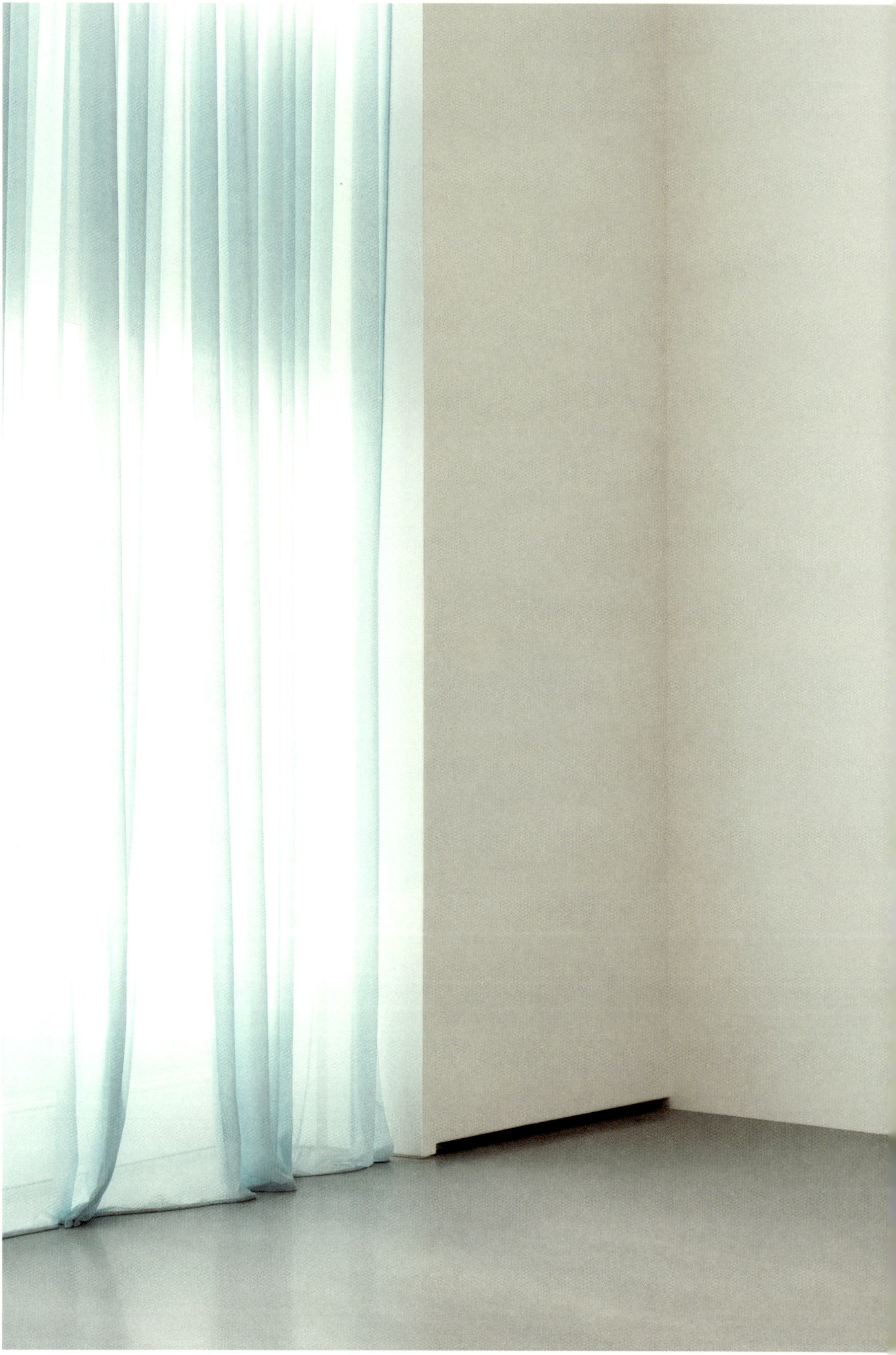

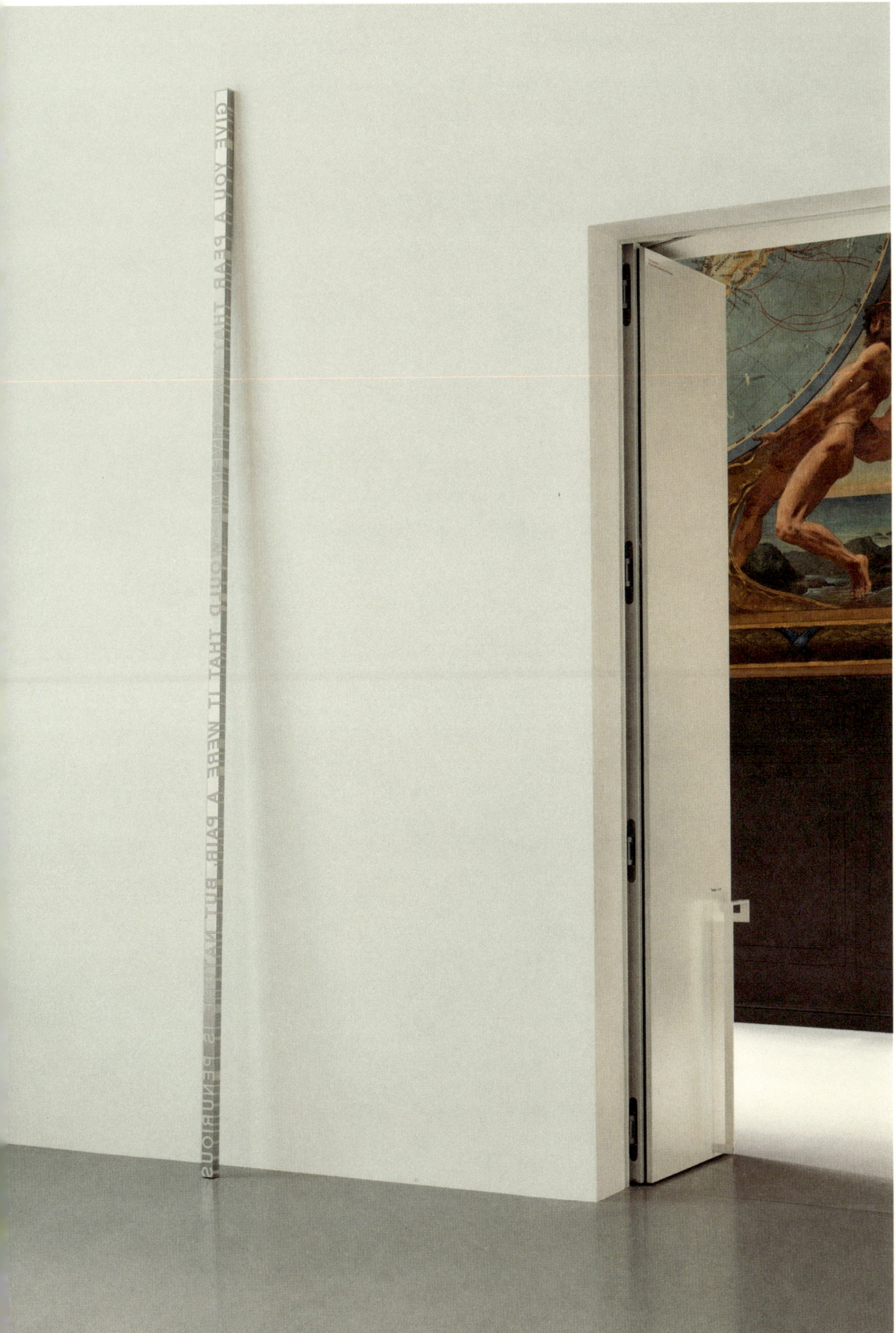

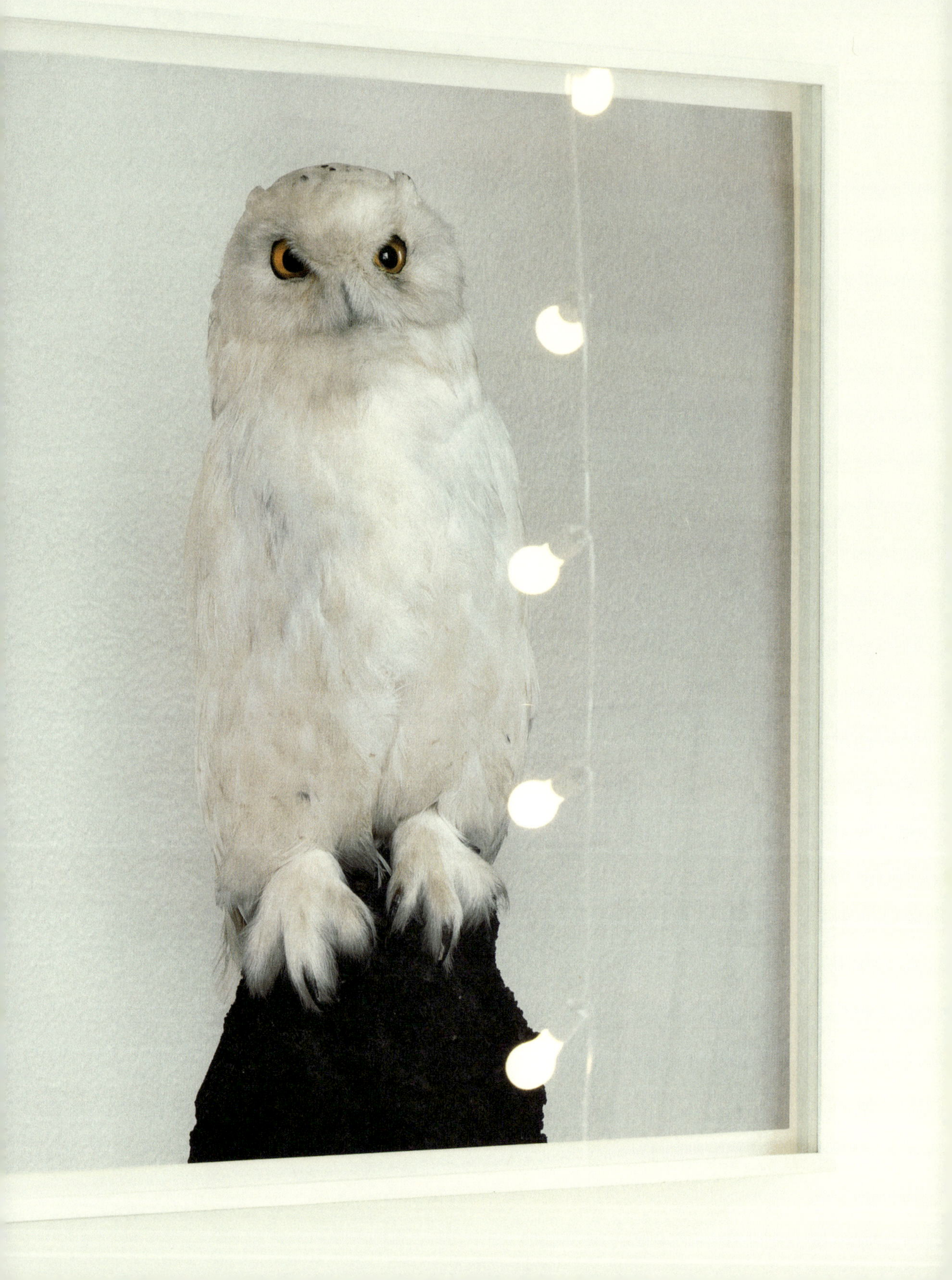

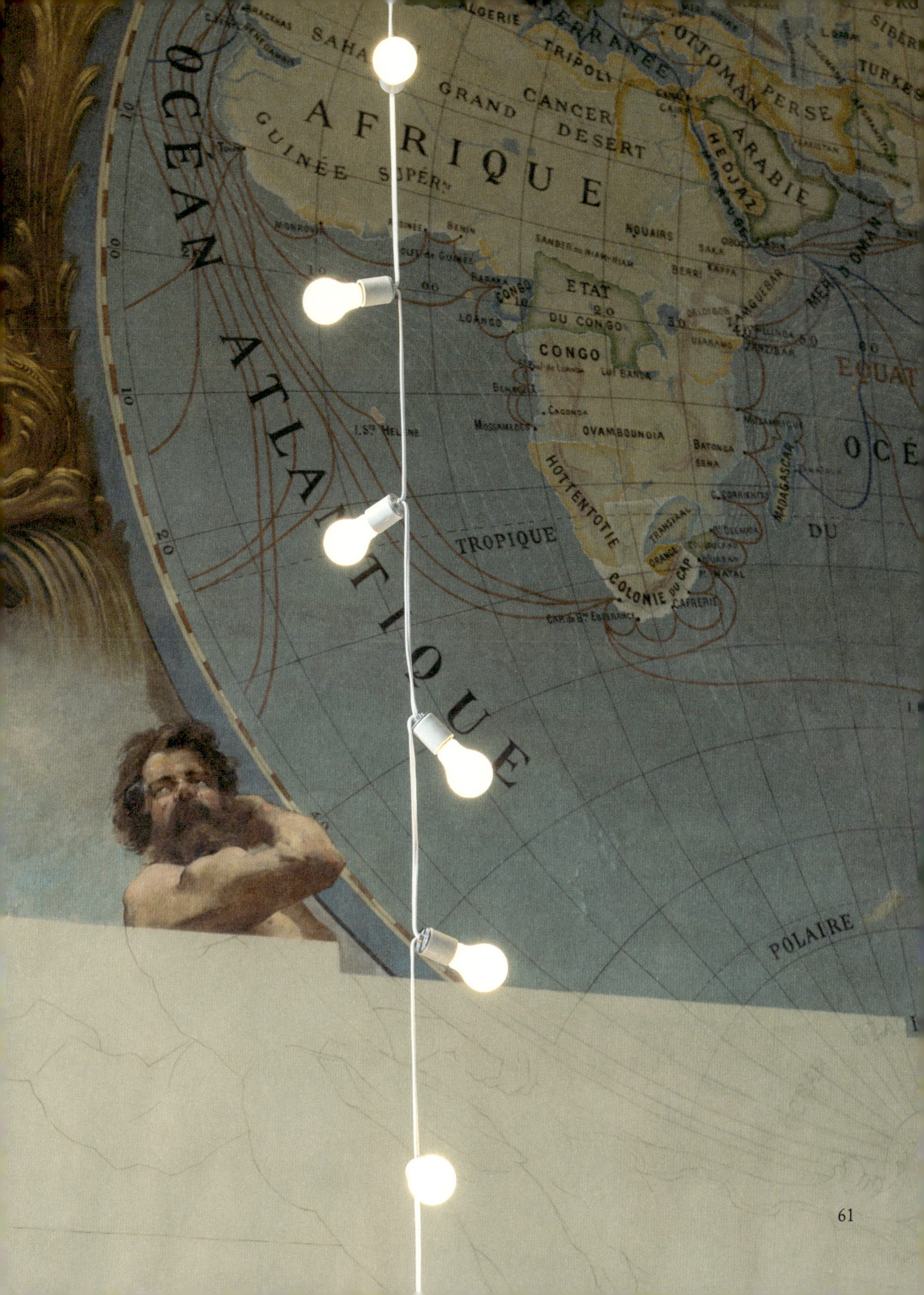
OCÉAN ATLANTIQUE
AFRIQUE
GUINÉE SUPÉR
GRAND
CANCER
DESERT
TRIPOLI
OTTOMAN
PERSE
ARABIE
HEDJAZ
ETAT DU CONGO
CONGO
LOANGO
BENIN
OVAMBOUNDIA
HOTTENTOTIE
TROPIQUE
TRANSVAAL
ORANGE
COLONIE DU CAP
CAFRERIE
NATAL
MADAGASCAR
ZANGUEBAR
DU
POLAIRE

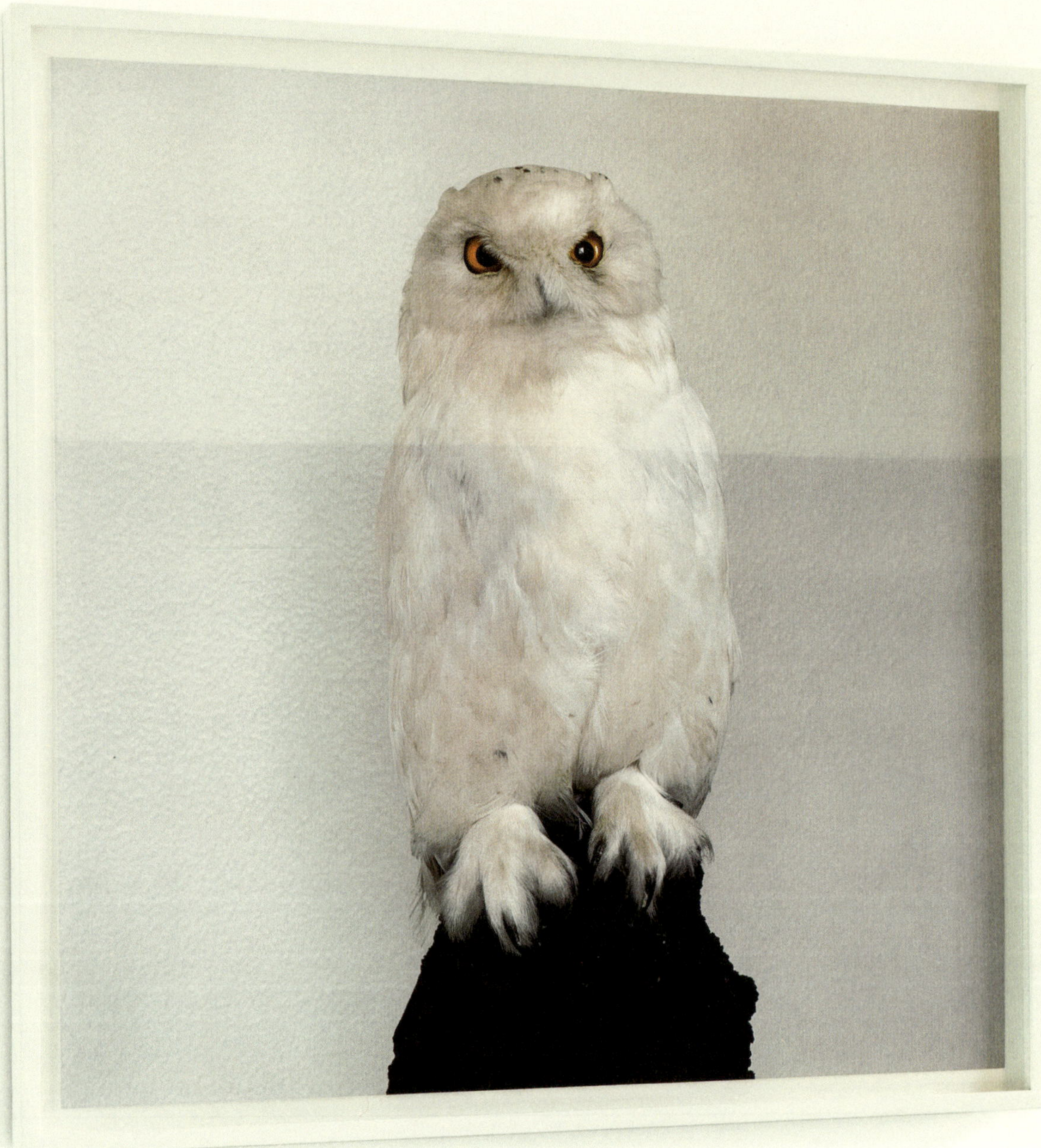

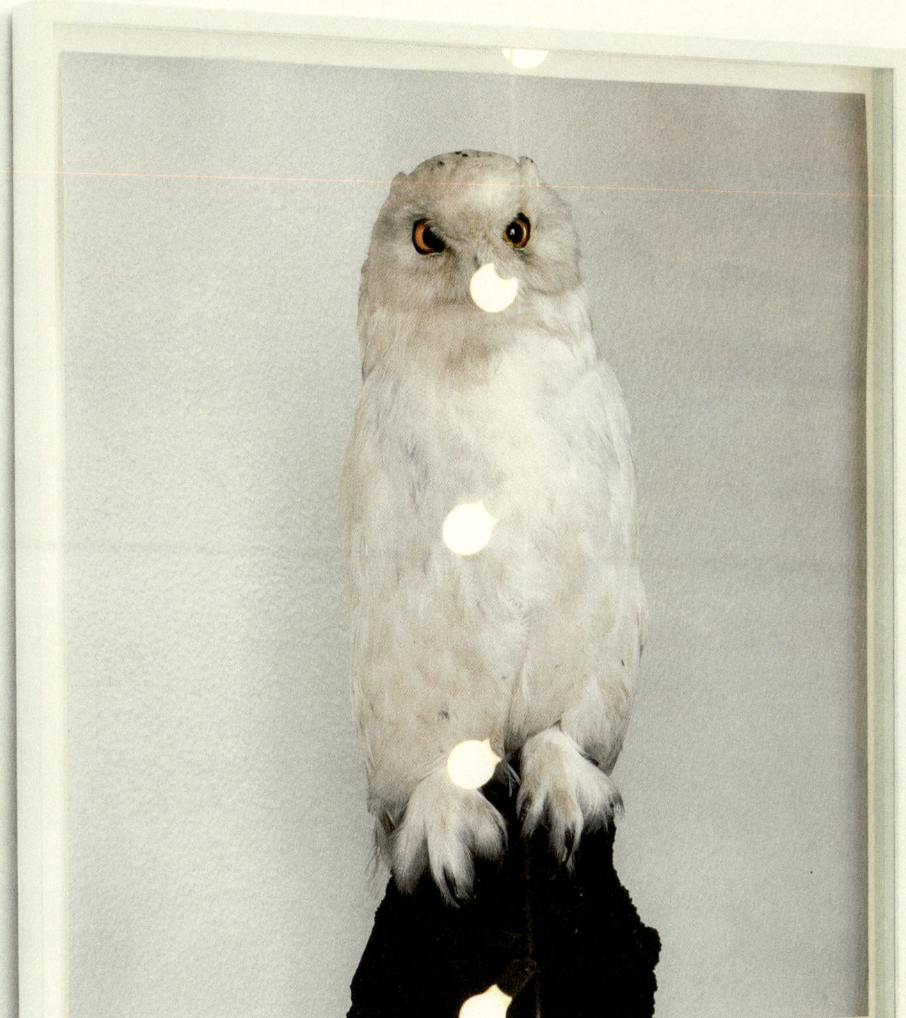

Félix González-Torres Roni Horn

▸ In Order of Appearance

FGT ***"Untitled" (Perfect Lovers),*** 1987-1990
Wall clocks / 2 parts / 34 cm / 13¼" diameter, each.

FGT ***"Untitled" (For Stockholm),*** 1992
Light bulbs, porcelain light sockets, electrical cords / 12 parts / Dimensions vary.

RH ***Well and Truly,*** 2009-2010
Solid cast glass with as-cast surfaces / 10 parts / 45.7 x 91.5 cm / 18 x 36" dia. ea.

FGT ***"Untitled" (Blood),*** 1992
Strands of beads, hanging device / Dimensions vary.

RH ***Double Möbius,* v. 2,** 2009/2018
'4 nine' pure gold foil / 2 ribbons, pegs / 76.2 x 15 x 15 cm / 30 x 6 x 6" as installed.

RH ***White Dickinson*** **HE INHERITS HIS UNCLE EMILY'S ARDOR FOR THE LIE,** 2006-2007
Solid aluminum, cast plastic / 226.7 x 5.1 x 5.1 cm / 89¼ x 2 x 2".

FGT ***"Untitled" (Loverboy),*** 1989
Sheer blue fabric, hanging device / Dimensions vary.

RH ***Dog's Chorus–Let Slip Until the Cows Come Home,*** 2016
Watercolor, ink, graphite on paper / 3 parts / Framed 200 x 72.4 cm / 78¾ x 28½" overall.

RH ***a.k.a.,*** 2008-2009
Photographs / Inkjet prints on rag paper / 15 pairs / Framed 43.2 x 38 cm / 17 x 15" ea.

FGT ***"Untitled" (Orpheus, Twice),*** 1991
Mirrors / 2 parts / 195 x 70 cm / 76¾ x 27½" ea.

RH ***White Dickinson*** **I GIVE YOU A PEAR THAT WAS GIVEN ME – WOULD THAT IT *WERE* A WPAIR, BUT NATURE IS PENURIOUS,** 2006-2007
Solid aluminum, cast plastic / 428.3 x 5.1 x 5.1 cm /168½ x 2 x 2".

FGT ***"Untitled" (Passport),*** 1991
Paper, Endless supply / 10 x 60 x 60 cm / 4 x 23½ x 23½".

RH ***Deal Owl,*** 1997
Photographs / Iris prints on rag paper / 2 parts / Framed 77.5 x 77.5 cm / 30½ x 30½" ea.

An Undiscovered Ocean Julie Ault

Intimate traces. Everybody. Nearby. Glowing in the light. Melting in the mouth. Reflecting. Pooling. Multiplied. Elapsing. Puzzled. Piled. Parting the curtain. Flowing. Emitting. Coupled. Soaring in the sky. Publicized. Becoming. Materialized. Illuminated. Layered. Crosscut. Imprinted. In the wings. Tucked away. Paired. Metabolized. Remembered. Shimmering. Absorbing. Mirroring. Embracing. Doubled. Forecast. Vanished. Conjoined. Glistening in the sea. Replenished.

Dwelling in possibility.

Like clocks, dead owls observe without judgment.

Infinite looping.

Revolving on itself indefinitely.

Enduring and ephemeral.

Waiting for the right viewer willing and needing to be moved to a place of the imagination.

A Möbius-like totality.

Right here, right now.

We were blown away by the heroic, gentle and horizontal presence of this gift.

A constellation and its interactions.

EXPANSE CANNOT BE LOST

Passport's stack of blank paper near words made solid on a lustrous beam.

She spoke to me most clearly and directly in the shadowy spaces behind her words.

Transfigured, deformed, recast, dispersed. Don't expect to find your bearings here. Phrases fracture, join and reconfigure. Severed, lacerated, distressed, shattered, dismembered, slivered, dissected. Letters and words strain to retain their shape.

Unknown forms.

The liquid words seem now in agitated, shimmering movement, the doubling suggesting the distortions we see in reflections in water.

Embodied metaphysics.

Parallel mirrors seem to absorb what they reflect.

An undiscovered ocean.

The doors through which Death comes and goes.

Virtual images appear and vanish with every move and glance.

This quality of presence requires unity between outside and inside, between visible and non-visible.

Spectral streams of light.

Elusiveness should be allowed to elude.

Light is absorbed or reflected in various ways depending on an object's texture and transparency. Specular reflection–light rebounds from a smooth surface at a definite angle–mirrorlike; diffuse reflection occurs along a vast array of angles in all directions; multiple reflection, the back and forth of light between reflective surfaces.

A mediating presence.

Sharp shapes and likenesses gradually yield nebulous visions. Mirage-like blurs ripple and evaporate.

Reflections concentrate and mingle, untraceable.

Expanding affinity.

Every moment is a present moment.

Pooled sensibilities.

A continuous process of becoming and mutability.

Liquid distortions.

For me water is a mentor.

Proof of resemblance to her multitudinous self.

A compilation of histories, past, present, and future, always, always shifting, adding, subtracting, gaining.

Through the medium of time, as if through water, breathing herself in and out as we do oxygen.

A plurality of perspective and experience. Be here now.

Translucent blue curtains veil high windows.

Immersed in depths. Boundless.

We are always new.

Up close and distant. Across boundaries.

Water memory. Undercurrent.

Harmonic communion.

No inside, outside, front, back, beginning, or end.

Unorientable.

Mirroring and emanating light.

Double Möbius. The gold continuum.

Physical and metaphysical infinities.

Ignited and suffused.

Gold ribbon that you are

Félix as ambient light.

Looking upon, looking through, looking into.
Layered views. Layers of you. Layers of view.

To be absorbed into the world as itself a form of becoming, to become part of others' being limitlessly, forever.

An invitation to enter a world of shadows.

Dangling strands of red beads choreographed to form a shimmering passport.

To be installed in a doorway, passageway, or other location through which people would naturally pass.

The bead strands actively sway when passed through and uniformly return to resting.

Blood remembering.

Subversive beauty.

A new landscape, a possible horizon, a place of rest and absolute beauty.

The paradox of glass. A viscous liquid, an amorphous solid.

Imperceptibly in motion.

On the floor, along the walls, throughout, in the mirrors, through the windows.

Reflections of reflections.

Moves in and out of object and event, illumination throughout everything in the show. It's a kind of sunlight in that it's pervasive.

Symbiotic. Winding. Surrounding. Flowing. Aglow.

When light traveling through air encounters a glass boundary, a portion of the light refracts, and some of it is reflected in the glass.

Internal reflection.

To me, the beauty of art lies in this dynamic with the viewer, which gives rise to a truly intimate and precise opportunity.

Every gaze into the glassy surfaces renders particular sights and depths.

Incandescence spills into arctic blue planes. Liquid identity. Chromaticity.

The clarifying function of relation.

A drawing in active dialogue with this particular location. The sense of place it creates, its relationship to the atmosphere, light, architecture, history, and traffic moving through. It interacts with the ambient setting like a landscape.

Spaciously dispersed. Spontaneous, decentered, episodic, asymmetrical.

Collaborating with sunlight.

Sitting on the floor, ever so lightly.

Well and Truly. Ten parts, solid cast glass in ten unique shades of blue.

Molten glass is poured into a mold and gradually cooled until the molecular movement all but ceases. The new matter is more organized than a liquid but less ordered than a crystalline solid. Disorganized solids flow exceptionally slowly.

The shiny surface is naturally polished by the heat from the furnace. *It's part of the organic reality of the glass.*

Like a ghost image from the adjacent room, the blue glass beams a reflection in the same ethereal hue.

In my mind's eye, the diaphanous sky blues meet gleaming glacial hues.

Informalism.

This is not some minimalist artwork that has to be exactly two inches to the left and six inches down. Play with it, please. Have fun. Give yourself that freedom. Put my creativity into question, minimize the preciousness of the piece . . .

Strings of cascading light bulbs pool on the floor.

Light produced by heat. *An incandescent light bulb is a controlled fire on display.*

My own history of light.

"Untitled" (For Stockholm).

The work may be displayed in a different configuration each time it is installed. The piece is completed upon the owner's or borrower's unique choice of installation.

Intimate traces.

Everybody.

Nearby.

Glowing in the light.

Reflecting.

Pooling. Multiplied.

Elapsing.

Tucked away.

Paired.

Metabolized. Remembered.

Mirroring.

Vanished.

Replenished.

Two clocks maintain an enduring duet.

Once molten.

An ever-changing atmosphere, resolving in daylight.

* Quotations in italics: Félix González-Torres, Roni Horn, FGT, FGT, Emily Dickinson, bell hooks, Briony Fer, FGT, Jean Cocteau, RH, RH, RH, RH, FGT, Dave Hickey, RH, RH, FGT, RH, Anne Carson, RH, Miwon Kwon, bell hooks, FGT, FGT, bell hooks, FGT, RH, RH, RH, FGT, RH, FGT, Regency Lighting, FGT, FGT.

Félix González-Torres Roni Horn
La Collection Pinault à la Bourse de Commerce, Paris
April 4 – September 26, 2022

COLOPHON

Thanks to
Julie Ault
Caroline Bourgeois
François Pinault
Gerhard Steidl
Dr. Jean Pierre Tarot

To collectors and institutions for lending work
Defares Collection
Ursula Hauser Collection
Marieluise Hessel Collection, Hessel Museum of Art, Center for Curatorial Studies, Bard College, Annandale-on-Hudson, New York
Musée d'Art moderne de Paris

And to
Karen Kelly, Abby Merrick, Monte Packham, Lukas Willen

Photography
Roni Horn with Marc Domage, Paris – pp. 12, 13, 16-19, 22-28, 30, 31, 36-38, 49, 51, 52, 57-63.
Roni Horn Studio, New York – pp. 29, 40.
Heinz Peter Knes, Berlin – pp. 7-11, 14, 15, 20, 32-35, 39, 41-48, 50, 53-56, front and back covers.
Aurélien Mole, Paris – pp. 21.

Photography Courtesy of
La Collection Pinault à la Bourse de Commerce, Paris

Book Concept and Design
Roni Horn Studio, New York

Color Correction and Prepress
Lena Beisert, Bernard Fischer, Judith Lange, and Reiner Motz, Göttingen

Printing
Steidl, Göttingen

Steidl
Düstere Str. 4 / 37073 Göttingen, Germany
Phone +49 551 49 60 60
mail@steidl.de
steidl.de

ISBN 978-3-96999-179-4
Printed in Germany by Steidl